Patroons & Periaguas

STUDIES IN MARITIME HISTORY

William N. Still, Jr., Series Editor

RECENT TITLES

Iron Afloat: The Story of the Confederate Armorclads
William N. Still, Jr.

To California by Sea: A Maritime History of the Gold Rush
James P. Delgado

Lifeline of the Confederacy: Blockade Running during the Civil War
Stephen R. Wise

The Lure of Neptune: German-Soviet Naval Collaboration and Ambitions
Tobias R. Philbin III

High Seas Confederate: The Life and Times of John Newland Maffitt
Royce Shingleton

The Defeat of the German U-Boats: The Battle of the Atlantic
David Syrett

John P. Holland, 1841–1914: Inventor of the Modern Submarine
Richard Knowles Morris

Cockburn and the British Navy in Transition: Admiral Sir George Cockburn, 1772–1853
Roger Morriss

The Royal Navy in European Waters during the American Revolutionary War
David Syrett

Sir John Fisher's Naval Revolution
Nicholas A. Lambert

Forty-Niners 'round the Horn
Charles R. Schultz

The Abandoned Ocean
Andrew Gibson and Arthur Donovan

Northern Naval Superiority and the Economics of the American Civil War
David G. Surdam

Ironclads and Big Guns of the Confederacy: The Journal and Letters of John M. Brooke
Edited by George M. Brooke, Jr.

High Seas and Yankee Gunboats: A Blockade-Running Adventure from the Diary of James Dickson
Roger S. Durham

Dead Men Tell No Tales: The Lives and Legends of the Pirate Charles Gibbs
Joseph Gibbs

Playships of the World: The Naval Diaries of Admiral Dan Gallery, 1920–1924
Edited by Robert Shenk

Captains Contentious: The Dysfunctional Sons of the Brine
Louis Arthur Norton

Lewis Coolidge and the Voyage of the Amethyst*, 1806–1811*
Evabeth Miller Kienast and John Phillip Felt

Promotion—or the Bottom of the River
John M. Stickney

Patroons and Periaguas: Enslaved Watermen and Watercraft of the Lowcountry
Lynn B. Harris

Patroons & Periaguas

Enslaved Watermen and Watercraft of the Lowcountry

Lynn B. Harris

The University of South Carolina Press

Published by the University of South Carolina Press
Columbia, South Carolina 29208

www.uscpress.com

Manufactured in the United States of America

31 30 29 28 27 26 25 24 23 22 10 9 8 7 6 5 4 3 2

Library of Congress Cataloging-in-Publication Data

Harris, Lynn B.
Patroons and periaguas : enslaved watermen and watercraft of the lowcountry / Lynn B. Harris.
pages cm
Includes bibliographical references and index.
ISBN 978-1-61117-385-7 (hardback) — ISBN 978-1-61117-386-4 (ebook) 1. Charleston County (S.C.)—Social life and customs—18th century. 2. Boatbuilders—South Carolina—Charleston County. 3. Navigation—History—18th century. 4. Cultural pluralism—South Carolina—Charleston County. 5. Charleston County (S.C.)—Antiquities. 6. Charleston County (S.C.)—History—18th century. 7. Plantation life—South Carolina—Charleston County. 8. Boatmen—South Carolina—Charleston County. 9. Slaves—South Carolina—Charleston County—History—18th century. I. Title.
F277.C4H36 2014
975.7'9102—dc23 2014004298

Contents

Illustrations

Preface

As we motored slowly past alligators sunning on banks of the murky orange-brown Cooper River, our mission to investigate an underwater site near a plantation, my underwater archaeologist colleagues and I speculated about the origins of these remnants of boats and ships scattered on the riverbed. Who had built and used these waterlogged relics, referred to so prolifically in colonial literature as periaguas?[1] The South Carolina frontier, from a European point of view, was a wild world where watermen of diverse ethnicities shared, adopted, and adapted aquatic skills to survive. They crewed together as an informal colonial navy in galleys guarding the mouths of the Edisto, Kiawah, and Savannah Rivers, rowed and raced plantation boats, swam proficiently, fought alligators, fished for profits, and worked side by side as laborers in large shipyards.

Historical manuscripts such as letters, logbooks, plats, probate records, photographic images, newspaper editorials, and remnants of material culture stored in museum sheds and embedded in marshes and on riverbeds yield tantalizing clues and stories surrounding these activities and interactions. Enslaved watermen built and ran away in plantation boats, boarded ships in port as crew to West Indies, and hired out to shipyards to learn shipwright skills displacing frustrated white laborers seeking employment. Enslaved patroons (captains) and their crews provided an invaluable service to planters, yet were also the linchpins for networks of river communications and illegal trade. "PS. Don't let the boat Negroes go amongst the Plantation Negroes," the plantation owner Henry Laurens frequently admonished his slave overseers Timothy Creamer and John Smith at Mepkin Plantation.[2] The statutes of South Carolina reflect efforts to regulate the independence of slave boatmen. As early as 1696 an "Act to Prevent the Stealing and the Taking away of Boats and Canoes" was passed, threatening any slave who "shall take away or let loose any boat, perriager or canoe or take away any grappling, painter, rope, sail or oar from any landing or place whatsoever" with thirty-nine lashes for the first offense and loss of an ear for repetition.[3] Yet, a petition about trade and coastal defense addressed to the

English monarch by merchants and planters of South Carolina and Georgia describes a crisis in the colonies, where there was "upwards of four blacks to one white person."[4]

Maritime history is usually taught with a Eurocentric focus on large ships of war, trade exploration, and the design evolution of hull shapes and machinery. Scholars like Peter Wood, Jeffrey Bolster, Marcus Rediker, David Cecelski, and Kevin Dawson highlight the neglected contributions of Native Americans and Africans to inland and coastal aquatic endeavors.[5] Leland Ferguson's provocative book *Uncommon Ground* is an early landmark study that addresses the role of plantation slaves in South Carolina as potters who retained their cultural traditions and made a low-fired, burnished pottery, occasionally marked with "X," that was used in spiritual rituals linked to the river, as was done in communities in Africa.[6] Since then, scholars studying other archaeological sites have suggested that this pottery was not exclusive to Africans but rather a creole product with a mixture of stylistic attributes, suggesting it was made by both Native Americans and early European settlers. Archaeologists recovered some of this pottery from plantations sites in proximity to sites where we conducted underwater archaeological investigations.

As in the "colonoware" pottery debates, there is a more complex maritime history to be tackled—that of a shared or creole maritime heritage in South Carolina. As people came together, society was repeatedly categorized in official records and surveys as comprising "negroes, mulattoes, mustees, and Indian" rather than white and black or European, Indian, and African.[7] Equally important to their new ethnic constructs and perceptions about demographics and natural resources was the array of skills people brought to the table from their respective homelands or assimilated from one another, including boat- and shipbuilding, swimming, boat handling, fishing, and piloting. It was an intricately woven cultural tapestry of maritime contributions from the former cultures of the immigrants and their occupational groups, with social boundaries that were often fluid through time and space.

Because Charleston was a colonial seaport, strategically situated at the congruence of two major river arteries, it drew a steady influx of diverse cultural groups that developed strong vested interests in boating and seafaring. The rivers leading into the port were essentially the roads of a bygone era for these early waves of immigrants. Settlement patterns of South Carolina were determined by the rivers and by coastal geography. Not only was the soil more fertile near the rivers, but the necessity of transporting agricultural goods made river frontage property extremely valuable and required ships built by immigrant shipwrights and their shipyard slaves to fit certain draft and design specifications.[8] Newspapers announcing ship launchings or boat sales describe intricate details of the ships' construction and design and specified the inclusion of local materials suited to the environment and to use in West Indies trade. For example, in 1763 the construction of a ship was described thus: a "length of keel, 27½ feet, strait rabbit, 11 feet beam or better, a shallow square tuck about 13 inches deep, the head of the stern post before the rudder café in the cockpit is cedar, . . . the new mainmast of this country pine, the foremast a Northward spruce pine, the bowsprit the country pine, with a great many worm holes in it, her boot-tops are painted with white lead and oil, her bends black, sides yellow, counter red, quarters and stern green, timber heads and crutches vermillion red, and inside Spanish brown."[9]

The maritime history of this cosmopolitan seaport and its waterway parish and plantation community clusters is more appropriately tackled from a synthetic viewpoint, similarly to studies of early language roots, contact, and creolization.[10] Another similar analytical framework is that of a Southern culture developing from various folk cultures of uprooted Africans and Britons. It started with the first settlers and continued through time as they attempted to adjust their respective cultural traditions and material culture to those of one another.[11] Culture in the New World was a "continuing series of reciprocal relationships involving borrowing, resistance, conflict, cooperation, modification and invention." It was an ongoing, dynamic process of different peoples adapting to one another and their New World that is central to our understanding, as scholars, of the South Carolina maritime cultural landscape. It was not a static relationship but one that changed constantly through time as people drew and redrew social boundaries in an effort to exercise some degree of control over specific events, the environment, and new waves of arriving immigrants.[12]

This book explores the creole maritime legacy of people who established communities along the rivers and in a shipyard with enslaved mariners and craftsmen as central figures in the narrative. Examining these interactions provides both a complementary and a different understanding of colonial society viewed against other aspects of Southern culture studied by scholars in areas such as house architecture, rice cultivation, pottery, and food preparation, all of which took place within the context of river transportation. Investigating activities around water and upon watercraft has the potential to offer new insights into colonial-era economic, social, and labor history. River mariners' cultural contributions are a less-explored aspect of plantation history, in contrast to studies of slave boatmen as fugitives and runaways. Incorporating interdisciplinary evidence—archaeological case studies, artwork, and historical vignettes—paints a more holistic and tangible picture of this local maritime legacy.

Acknowledgments

This book was inspired by my twelve years of employment with colleagues at the Underwater Archaeology Division (now the Maritime Research Division) at the South Carolina Institute of Archaeology and Anthropology. I had the great privilege of exploring and diving in some of the most beautiful rivers and sounds of South Carolina as part of my job. More important, I had the pleasure of meeting many divers, museum curators, archaeologists, and other South Carolinians who generously shared their knowledge, valuable insights, and time.

Special thanks to all the staff at special collections of the College of Charleston Library, the South Carolina Department of Archives and History, the South Caroliniana Library at the University of South Carolina, the South Carolina Historical Society, and the South Carolina room at the Charleston Public Library who helped me navigate my way through their collections.

I am especially thankful to my former and current colleagues at the history department of East Carolina University for giving me the time and encouragement to pursue this project. Finally, this effort would not have been possible with the support, patience, and the understanding of my family—Pat, Leigh, and Ben.

1.

The Colonial Cultural Landscape

In June 1666 Robert Sanford, an early settler and previously a planter in Barbados, reported to the Lord Proprietors that the Carolina coast had bountiful natural resources and that for "fertility of soyle, for excelancy of Rivers, havens, Creeks and sounds, for abundance of Timber of diverse sorts, and many other requisites to both land and Sea building, and for Sundry rare accomodacons both for Navigation and Plantacon [it] Exceed[s] all places that wee knowe in proporcon of our Nacon in the West Indies."[1] A century later a traveler in colonial South Carolina gave his first impressions of the landscape: "Most of the coast [of Carolina], for many miles within land, consists of low islands and extensive marshes, divided also by innumerable creeks and narrow muddy channels, thro which only boats, canoes, and periaguas can pass." He further explained that "those inland passages are of great use to the inhabitants, who without being exposed to the open sea, travel in safety in boats and periaguas."[2]

Throughout the colonial period, these waterways continued to symbolize the food ways and highways for Native Americans, a medley of European immigrants and their equally ethnically diverse African slaves. The landscape, as Sanford predicted, was ideal for providing raw materials to build and repair boats and ships for inland excursions as well as for the West Indies and European trading voyages. Inland waterways played a pivotal role in colonial contact situations that evolved between newcomers and indigenous peoples in South Carolina, contributing to the early survival of the colony. These pursuits included establishing hunting, fishing, and trading relationships; exploring a new environment; acquiring a labor force through slavery; and developing a security system to protect the coastline in addition to colonists' inland economic interests. In these initial endeavors, a valuable playing card was Native Americans'

Figure 1. Theodor de Bry's engraving depicting Indian men manufacturing a canoe. Permission of North Carolina Collection, University of North Carolina.

familiarity with local waterways and their ability to utilize and exploit it effectively, using expediently built local water craft. New settlers took every possible advantage of their boatbuilding and boat handling experience for navigating inland waters of the lowcountry.

Boats were traditionally one of Native Americans' most important possessions, for both past and contemporary societies in the larger southeastern region, such as the Seminole in Florida or the Embera of Panama. One young Embera man told a traveler that when he was growing up his father said, "You must know how to make a piragua [a large dugout canoe] or a canalete [the small dugout] for without this knowledge you cannot catch a woman. If you are in a big river, what will you cross in? How can you cut plantains or carry corn and rice?"[3] Spiritual qualities were linked to boats, and certain rituals were undertaken to ensure that the spirit of the tree did not became dissatisfied and angry during the manufacturing process. The boat was a symbol of life, security, and prosperity. Rivers were links to commerce and communication. Boats were absolutely essential to Native Americans' river-oriented life style. Europeans considered Charleston to be the colonial metropolis of the southern Indian frontier, and it was here that deerskin traders from the mountains and from the Gulf plains paid their annual business visits. Native Americans were not only trading partners but also the oarsmen or manufacturers of the early colonial trading water craft, constituting the bulk of the crews on scout boats patrolling the coastline. To the early explorers and plantation owners, Native American slaves were significant sources of information about trading, fishing, hunting, and canoe manufacturing and operating. Essentially, the interaction between the European newcomers and the inhabitants revolved around water, and therefore use of boats was a critical part of the equation.

The early accounts of boat usage in South Carolina are derived from the correspondence of the early Spanish exploration expeditions. In 1566, in the wake of the explorer Hernando de Soto, Juan Pardo, a Spanish captain, explored much of South Carolina. He and his men were dependent on Native American canoes to transport them across many of the rivers. Wherever they traveled, dugout canoes were their primary mode of transportation. They also traded iron tools, especially axes, chisels, and knives, to local chiefs in exchange for canoes constructed for them by the Native Americans and used the canoes specifically to explore the Southeast.[4] Descriptions of canoe usage are given in some of these early reports. The average canoe was so narrow that it was not to the liking of the Spaniards, and Francisco Villareal, a Jesuit missionary, complained that they frequently capsized. The Native Americans were agile, however, and could stand upright and pole them. Two colonial traveling artists, the Frenchman Jacques le Moyne and the Englishman John White, provide graphic evidence of the popularity of canoe usage. A painting by Jacques le Moyne shows three Timucuan Native Americans transporting food in a canoe. Three men paddle the boat in standing positions, while two women recline in the rear. The canoe appears to be extremely narrow, with shallow sides and square-shaped ends. Another painting by le Moyne shows a similar canoe with a small fire on board for warmth and light.[5]

A painting of an early engraving by Theodor de Bry, based on a painting executed around 1585 by John White, the official artist on a voyage to the Carolinas, carefully illustrates the method used by Native Americans to manufacture canoes. It depicts a canoe in the process of being burned and carved out of a large tree. The caption states that it was made "onely with the help of fire and hatchets of stone and shell" and specifies that a tall straight tree called "rackiock," perhaps cypress (*taxodium distichium*), was used to make canoes. Another drawing shows canoes ferrying goods to storage areas. Again the Native Americans are standing and poling.[6] An engraving of a fishing scene, based on another of John White's paintings, depicts a canoeist using a paddle with a rounded shovel-shaped blade. In the middle of the boat, two figures crouch over a fire. Standing in the stern, a fourth man uses a dip net. In the distant background, numerous other canoes and men wading in shallow water or standing poised to stick fish with a harpoon or spear are visible. The creatures shown in the water

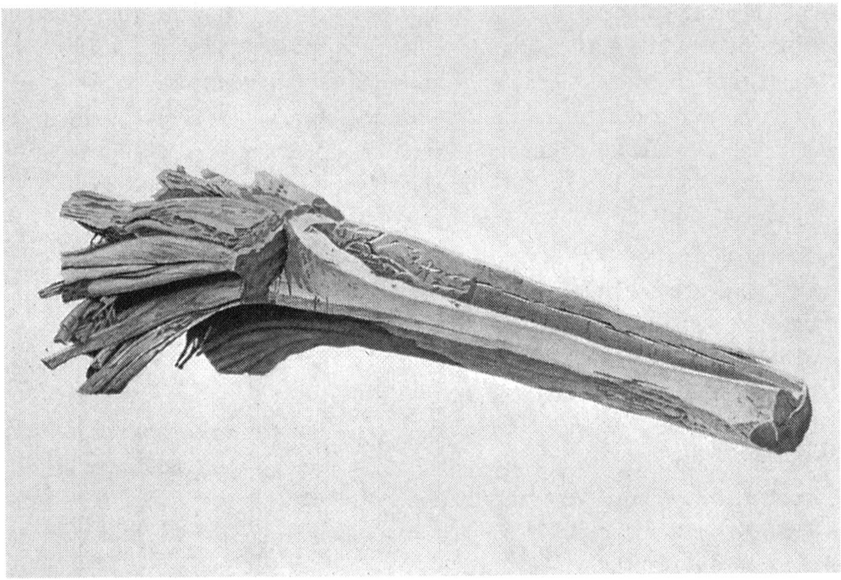

Figure 2. Roots canoe. Courtesy of SCIAA.

are varied and include a loggerhead turtle, a land crab, snake-like amphibians, and two fish weirs.

William Bartram, a pioneering ethnographer in South Carolina, described some of his perceptions of his first hosts and their boats: "they are supplied with necessaries, conveniences, and even superfluities by the white traders . . . men performing nothing except erecting mean habitations, forming their canoes, stone pipes, tambour, eagles tails . . . for war and hunting are their principal employments. . . . Women are more vigilant, and turn their attention to various manual employments . . . make all their pottery or earthenware, moccasins, spin and weave the curious belts and diadems for men."[7] Bartram's rambling travel writings about flora, fauna, and the inhabitants include numerous references to transportation modes, both his and those of Native Americans en route. Fish, especially bream, Bartram's favorite kind, were welcome gifts from Native Americans whom he met in their fishing canoes. He expressed his surprise that the daily catch was of such quantity and variety. In Florida he described how "Indians have large handsome canoes . . . some of them commodious enough to accommodate twenty or thirty warriors. In these large canoes they descend the river on trading and hunting expeditions to the seacoast, neighboring islands and keys, and sometimes cross the gulph, extending their navigations to the Bahama Islands and even to Cuba."[8] On occasion, under the pretense of a brief fishing excursion, Bartram borrowed canoes from Native Americans and made trips of six or seven miles up and down local rivers. When he had to cross a body of water without a canoe, he and his crew constructed temporary rafts by using vine to tie together several tree trunks. Two vines were placed at either end to pull the rafts across the river. To execute a crossing on one occasion, "the Indian took one end of one of the vines in his mouth, plunged into the river, and swam over with it."[9]

Evidence from archaeological excavations in South Carolina demonstrates that aquatic resources played a major role in diets of Native Americans. The canoe provided a platform for spearing fish with sharpened reeds, inspecting trotlines, removing fish from weirs, pearl diving and dip-netting. When the Native Americans lit a fire in a clay basin placed inside a canoe, the glow illuminated the water at night, attracting and dazzling fish that came to the surface. On certain occasions, entire families joined expeditions, carrying their furs and smoked meat inside canoes. Woman canoeists were also of great interest to John Lawson, who wrote that "many of the women are very handy in the canoes and manage them with great dexterity and skill."[10] These local Native American communities supplied fish to colonists and fished with them. Maurice Mathews, a settler, elaborated: "In all parts of the rivers and creeks, wee never want fish of several sorts which wee and our Indians do catch with netts, hooks, weirs, and by shooting them with arrows. The fish wee have are sturgeon, bass, drum, mullet, plaice, trouts, jacks, and catfish."[11] Another report described the "cockles, mussles, and Banks, nay Mountains of Oysters (and some with Pearl) that seem to brocade the creeks. Besides prodigious prawns and shrimps in the brackish and salt waters, but crawfish in the freshes; which are various entertainments, both to the native and the fortunate planter."[12]

Hunting, like boatbuilding, was an integral part of Native American culture. Successful hunting prowess improved a man's ability to attract a mate. Commenting on the Etiwan, a settler observed that "the prettiest girl always bestows upon the chieftest sports-man." Cherokee women also considered a man's hunting skills when looking for a mate. Hunting and fishing expedition were usually followed by feasting and celebration.[13] William Bartram described his encounter with a Native American who informed him that he lived at the next plantation, where he was employed a hunter. Archaeological research and historical accounts across the South indicate that slaves consumed a variety of domesticated animals, including beef, poultry, pork, sheep, and goat. Along the South Carolina and Georgia coasts, meat sources for slave diets diverged from this pattern by including turtles, fish, raccoons, rabbits, opossums, and deer.[14]

An English agriculturalist remarked "one Indian, or dextrous negroe, with his gun and netts, gets as much game and fish, as five families can eat." Slaves in South Carolina supplemented their diets through hunting and fishing. Who could be better than a skilled local hunter at procuring these foods and introducing the new immigrants to the most successful hunting and fishing techniques? Many food forays entailed the use of boats. Early sketches of life in the South Carolina lowcountry described "the custom of the planters to engage the services of an Indian hunter for less than 20 shillings a year, who could supply a family of thirty persons with as much venison and fowl as they can eat."[15]

The colonial naturalist and illustrator Mark Catesbury described several examples of cooperative European and Native American hunting and fishing expeditions. Five Native Americans and three white men set out to hunt at a location near Savannah River, returning in boats loaded with skins and fish and sharing fishing customs with one another. The group fished for drum in April and May, using the Native American practice of lighting fires in their canoes to attract the fish and then striking them with harpoons. Fish were barreled up with salt and sent to the West Indies. As the spring approached each year, sturgeon came into the estuaries and rivers to spawn. The inhabitants of Carolina, as the Native Americans had taught them, placed their canoes and boats strategically so that when the sturgeon leaped, they fell into the boat. At the end of summer, fish migrated upriver to the more rocky parts of the rivers, and "the English and Indians go to strike them . . . with a cane 14 feet in length . . . with this the striker stands at the head of the canoe and another steering it."[16]

Establishing profitable relationships based on Native Americans' knowledge of river routes was crucial information to newly arriving immigrants. Merchants used waterways as trade routes, and indigenous boats designs were the most functional and easily available. Native Americans served as trade boat labor and primary communicators, helping to develop networks of trade partnerships. Trade, the primary economic focus of the early settlement, was greatly enhanced by fostering Native American allies and trade partners. On June 28, 1699, Tho Culter wrote to the Lord Commissioners for Trade and Plantations that he had procured an "Indian trader and hunter to go upcountry."[17] Another letter that same year to the Lords by Edward Randolph explained that "a great Indian Trader" was willing to explore the country west from Charleston. The trader was asking for a payment of not above "400 or 500 pounds at most he intends to take with him white men of this province and two Indians."[18] Deerskins, furs, and Indian slaves were the most lucrative sources of trade between early European settlers and Native American men.[19] Other popular trade items were multicolored split wood and cane baskets, which demanded high prices. Trade goods acquired from Native American women tended to be subsistence goods, such as foodstuffs and livestock. Goods traded to Native Americans included guns for hunting, iron pots, hoes, mirrors, glass and pottery fragments, and cloth. Often direct substitutions were made—bullets for arrows, iron tomahawks for stone tomahawks, or colored cloth for more traditional dyed cloth.[20] Canoes continually hauled harvests of wild fruit and agricultural produce, connecting inland Native American groups or ferrying belongings and European explorers up and down the river. In certain instances, canoes may have had special significance. The official welcome given to de Soto's expedition by the Cofitachequi was delivered by a woman—"Cacia, the Lady of Cofitachequi." This important community representative arrived on a litter draped with delicate white cloth and placed in a canoe. Over the stern "was spread an awning, and in the bottom, lay extended a mat, where there were two cushions, one above the other, where she sat, and she was accompanied by her chief men." When she had crossed the river in her canoe, she presented the expedition with traditional clothing and skins carried in accompanying boats. Drawing a string of pearls over her head, she threw them over the expedition leader's neck, exchanging gestures of friendship and courtesy.[21]

Although there are no historical accounts of canoe warfare among the Indian peoples in South Carolina, in the Lower Mississippi River basin Native Americans attacked the survivors of de Soto's expedition. The largest canoes were propelled by twenty-five paddlers on each side and carried thirty additional warriors. Sheltering the paddlers with their shields, the warriors did not row but stood poised to shoot their arrows. Singing rhythmic songs as they paddled, the paddlers propelled their canoes to a speed comparable to that of a running horse. Some canoes were painted with the same color patterns as the warriors' clothing and weapons. Displaying a high level of expertise in water warfare, the paddlers split their flotilla into three groups to criss-cross the river in a coordinated attack on the Europeans.[22]

Native Americans used several types of watercraft along the southeastern seaboard. The easiest and quickest way to cross an unexpectedly deep waterway was simply to make a raft by lashing cane or logs together. Another method was to bind two or three bundles of cane together with straps. More time-consuming watercraft manufacturing processes entailed stretching skins of animals over a bowl-shaped framework of saplings, hollowing out a large log to form a dugout canoe, or creating a sort of catamaran by lashing two dugouts side by side. Poles laid across these two canoes created a platform, providing more cargo space. Some coastal dugouts had structural additions for masts and sails. Canoes also varied in size and design depending on the body of water to be navigated.[23]

Makers used a variety of woods for canoes. A controlled fire within the interior of a large shaped log facilitated hollowing, since it was easier to scrape out charred remnants than to remove unburned wood. In Carolina, pine, tulip, and cottonwood trees were most often utilized. Pine was probably chosen over cypress because pine resin was a natural igniting substance. Other reasons for using a particular wood included preference, tradition, and, in some areas, availability. Canoe makers chose cypress over pine when iron tools and, possibly, glass fragments became available and replaced the fire-hollowing technique and the use of shells or stone tools Almost all Florida groups used cypress, as did Seminoles up to the 1950s, using hatchets, adzes, and pocket knives. Ethnographic data were gathered by interviewing and observing one individual, Charlie Cypress, who detailed the entire process. Until the shaping process was almost complete, both ends of the canoe were not severed from the tree. One of the most interesting techniques observed by "white men" involving making holes with pocket knives in the bottom and sides of the tree trunk to estimate the thickness of the wood and to gauge the extent of the hollowing process. Before the canoe was placed in the water, Charlie Cypress inserted plugs in the holes and smoothed them so that they were level with the remainder of the bottom. He then completed the final finishing off with a special short-handled adze inherited from his father.[24]

Over time, canoe-style boats evolved as the transportation medium most appropriate for the coastal environments of colonial South Carolina. The easily manufactured and procured log watercraft facilitated trading activities on waterways, increasing contact, communication, and conflict among diverse ethnic groups.[25] Like Native Americans, newly arriving European settlers quickly realized benefits of living on waterways and saw the advantages of familiarizing themselves with geography of the rivers and the creek systems.

These early settlers came from many social classes, occupations, and geographic areas in Europe and West Indies. The most authoritative studies that explore the origins of early settlers who immigrated to South Carolina between 1670 and 1690 suggest that 54 percent of them were from Barbados. The great majority were from the small-planter and freehold classes, referring to small farmers owning at least ten acres of land but fewer than twenty slaves and freemen owning less than ten acres of land. Some emigrants from Barbados sold their property and used the proceeds to come to South Carolina, while others came as indentured servants. Those who came included the Barbadian elite, who owned at least sixty slaves. They were described as those who "held the best land, sold the most sugar, and monopolized the chief offices" on the islands. This social class included families such as the Middletons, Colletons, and Gibbses.[26]

Wealthier planter families brought the first African slaves from the West Indies to the Carolina colony.[27] English settlers came from almost all the counties of England and Wales, and seven counties of Ireland appear on lists of emigrants. At the same time that voluntary emigration was taking place, another type of exodus was ongoing. Oliver Cromwell, whose victories in England, Scotland, and Ireland encumbered him with prisoners of war, shipped his captives off to Barbados. By 1655, a total of 1,200 prisoners of war were alleged to be employed by the Barbados planters. This would have represented nearly half of the total white population on the island at the time, and many of these prisoners later re-emigrated to South Carolina.[28] The industrious Cromwell also began dispatching other "undesirables" to Barbados starting around 1654, including pirates caught on the high seas and "lewd, dangerous persons, rogues, vagrants, and idle persons."[29] French settlers included Huguenots attracted to South Carolina by the promise of religious and political freedom as well as by the availability of land. In 1680 a group of forty-five Huguenots arrived, and over the next few years others migrated as individuals or families. In 1685 Louis XIV revoked the Edict of Nantes, which had offered a measure of religious toleration to the Huguenots, and many persecuted French citizens fled in the following decade, with fifteen hundred arriving in South Carolina. Of the 326 Huguenots who arrived in Charleston between 1680 and 1700, 56 percent were born in the western coastal provinces of France.[30]

Many immigrants from the West Indies and Europe were listed as skilled artisans and laborers. A group that left Southampton was composed of "8 husbandmen, 2 sergeweavers, a hoopmaker, cordwayner, smith, ropemaker, barber, chandler, 2 shoemakers, seamen, curier, glover, and clotheworker."[31] A comprehensive study of immigrants who came to South Carolina between 1670 and 1700 lists their job titles; the list includes 108 mariners of all ranks, twenty-seven carpenters, and fifteen shipwrights. French settlers were also linked to a variety of trades such as goldsmith, blacksmith, shipwright, and carpenter.[32]

Until about 1696 practically every ship entering Charleston brought immigrants seeking new homes. While the majority remained in or near town, others pressed up river routes into the interior. Cooper River was a navigable river for almost thirty miles, and many newcomers in time took advantage of this, starting small settlements, farms, and plantations on both sides of the river. Various immigrant groups who arrived during the seventeenth century settled the lowcountry landscape in ethnic clusters along the river systems or around the harbor. They began to expand as far as the Santee, Wando, and Ashley Rivers, encountering Native American groups who also utilized the waterways. French settlements were scattered in an arc west, north, and east of Charleston, with the largest cluster noted along the south bank of the Santee. Many Barbadians settled between the Cooper and Ashley Rivers in the Charleston area, while others moved upriver into present-day Berkeley County.[33] Of the settler groups, the Barbadians were probably the most seasoned by their experiences and exposure to diseases in the West Indies. They also had a better understanding of how to survive in a colonial environment with one foot in England and the other in South Carolina. In contrast, among those who found the environment most inhospitable was a group of Puritans from Massachusetts. In 1695 they established the town of Dorchester on the Ashley River but, because of the poor sandy soil, were ultimately unable to prosper or to compete within the local plantation economy.[34]

In the beginning, vessels from the Bahamas or Barbados or those belonging to friends and business partners serviced the colonies. The sloop *Three Brothers,* owned by the Colleton family of Barbados, served the needs of the colony. James, Peter, and Thomas Colleton also owned another sloop, *John and Thomas,* from Barbados that carried eighty people from Barbados and more from the Leeward Islands to South Carolina. *Carolina,* which belonged to the Lord Proprietors, also served as an early means of transport and, like other early trade vessels, it did the round trip, loading up with South Carolina timber to trade with Barbados and then taking on a load of sugar and sailing for England, where Captain Brayne promised to transport three hundred new settlers from England back to the colony.[35] By the late 1600s settlers evidently began building boats in Charleston. Maurice Mathews writes that "there have been several vessels built here and now three or four are upon stocks." Mention of stocks or blocks refer to the supporting framework upon which ships were built, indicating that these were not small craft but larger ships that were under construction. One of the first shipwrights to arrive in Charleston was Magus Popell of Barbados, who came over in 1679 as commander of the bark *Return.*[36] At this time, in the 1670s, the ketch was at the height of its popularity. Sloops also became popular in the Caribbean during the second half of the 1600s. These single-mast vessels had deeper hulls that worked better to windward and could outrun pursuers like pirates.[37]

Early records of the colony mention a variety of vessels defined by both their rig and their hull shapes, including sloops, pinks, ketches, galleys, brigs, a snow, a bark, a dogger, shallops, and ships. All these were familiar craft in the West Indies and the northern colonies.[38] Settlers who came from the northern colonies probably introduced European vessel designs adapted to a colonial setting in North America. These groups included the Puritans at Dorchester and a group of New Yorkers, possibly of Dutch background, who settled at the mouth of the Ashley River. Other groups, such as the French, some of whom came from locales where split-log boats were built, may have contributed specific regional ideas about boating and boatbuilding.[39] Many French settlers originated from east of Bayonne, an area with a strong Basque influence, where there was a tradition of the split dugout design on the River l'Adour. A study of traditional boats in North Carolina revealed that many construction techniques are best attributed to skills and carpentry concepts developed from split-dugout making, and John Lawson, an early traveler, made observations about the French along the Santee River building split-log boats.[40]

Groups of settlers who came to South Carolina from the Caribbean and the Bahamas or who had had visited Africa were familiar with the use of large log or dugout canoes prior to arriving in the lowcountry. Watercraft traveled between the West Indies islands and, occasionally, on the open sea. For the Carib and the Arawak, the "canoa" was vital. Columbus first learned the word during his contact with the Arawak, according to his journal entry. He described the watercraft as being "95 palmos [65 feet] long and beautifully made from a single log, and big enough to carry 150 people" and mentioned "boathouses" or canopies of thatch and wood to protect the crew from sun and water.[41] European traders used locally built watercraft to transport their slaves, wares, and merchants inland and along the African coast. Yams, livestock, and slaves were the most prominent cargo carried from the interior in northwestern Africa. At the Bight of Bonny, "barge canoes capable of carrying 120 persons" engaged in slaving expeditions that might return with 1,500 or 2,000 victims.[42]

When European traders began to operate along the West African coast starting at the end of the fifteenth century, a form of interaction began between two waterborne trading systems. One was based in the Atlantic and controlled by Europeans and connected Africa with other continents, and the other was operated by indigenous merchants and coastal communities. These traders made use of the inland trading routes on bodies of water such as African estuaries or lagoons, much like South Carolina's natural environment. European accounts provide a detailed picture of the lagoon trade, with canoes plying from Lagos to Porta Nova and Badagry in the west of the continent and to Ikorodu and Ikosi, the lagoon-side ports in the east. The Portuguese reported that canoes were operating in the lagoons east of Lagos in the late fifteenth century, and a Dutch account describes the lagoon as "all over full of Fishers netts fastened with stakes."[43]

Lagos was an important commercial center to which commercial goods were brought by canoes through the lagoons. In 1668, the Dutch were trading cotton cloths specifically with the Yoruba kingdom of Ijebu. This city was approachable by the River Ona, which early explorers thought was an inland continuation of the river Lagos and lagoon area.[44] Historians have relied heavily on the records of Atlantic ship captains, European slave agents, and South Carolina slave traders and owners for insights into the geographic origins of African slaves.[45] Seventy percent of those making up the early waves of slaves that came directly into Charleston were from Angola, situated north of present-day Namibia. Africans brought to South Carolina from the sugar plantations of Barbados, Jamaica, and the other Caribbean islands probably had been born along the Guinea coast between the Senegal and Niger Rivers. This high predominance of early West Africans in South Carolina fits with overall trends for slave acquisition. An African database consisting of 4,860 samples of mitochondrial DNA (mtDNA) includes 948 mtDNA from west-central Africa. Researchers compared these data with a publicly available database of 1,148 African Americans from the

United States comprising 1,053 mtDNA samples of sub-Saharan ancestry. The data reveal that 55 percent of the U.S. lineages have West African ancestry, with 41 percent originating from west-central or southwestern Africa. These results are remarkably similar to the most up-to-date analyses of the historical record. Philip Curtin estimated that 50 percent of North American slaves came from northwest Africa, 48 percent from west-central Africa, and just 2 percent from southeast Africa. A much more recent estimate suggests that 64 percent were from northwest Africa, 35 percent were from west-central Africa, and 1 percent were from southeastern Africa.[46]

Planters in Carolina and the Caribbean considered "rebellious and lazy" southwest Angolan and west-central Congo slaves to be less desirable than those who came from northwestern African regions. Slaves from the Guinea coast were more expensive than those from the Gold Coast, a factor that may have influenced some of the Carolina purchases. Yet, Gambian slaves from the upper coast of Guinea had more knowledge of rice growing, which was an important consideration to planters.[47] The slave owner Henry Laurens proclaimed that "it must be observed that these were all Gambia and Windward Coast cargoes [of slaves] which are better esteemed by our people than Angolas."[48] Planters believed that Senegambian slaves were harder working and offered less resistance to slavery. The ability of slaves from Congo and Angolan to speak Portuguese also point toward a greater level of cultural integration than occurred with slaves of colonists from other European nations and suggests that those from Barbados and Africa may have had some familiarity with Portuguese boat designs.[49]

While African and Native American material culture had closer ties to canoe-type inland or coastal boatbuilding, a key element of the nascent economy was oceangoing trade with the Caribbean islands, Europe, and Africa. Ships for this purpose, Europeans thought, were most suitably constructed under the supervision of a trained European shipwright. Although there were shipwrights among the early settlers, there was not a critical need to build oceangoing boats locally at the outset. Colonial officials devoted manpower to agricultural pursuits and experimental initiatives such as the deerskin trade. Early Carolinians relied on the vessels built in other colonies and in England for trade purposes and on the Royal Navy, which was already spread fairly thinly. What events, then, led South Carolinians to realize that there a financial edge to building their own offshore trading boats?

Successful experimentation with rice in the 1690s facilitated the accumulation of capital gains and, with that, the ability to purchase slave labor. As South Carolina settlers gradually overcame the harsh realities and seasoning of a pioneer existence—clearing land, cutting wood, and cultivating provisions—they started producing more goods for export. They saw a huge financial advantage in building, owning, and operating their boats instead of relying entirely on the British and West Indian vessels for carrying their trade.[50] It is difficult to assess the extent and importance of shipbuilding during the early years of the colony's history and impossible to guess how many vessels were built prior to 1690. Ship refitting occurred from the very start of the settlement. This was an era when every vessel entering port had to undergo some sort of overhaul to make it seaworthy, a task that could be done in the most primitive conditions. Shipbuilding, in contrast, required proper facilities and skilled craftsmen. Nevertheless, it appears that in the last two decades of the seventeenth century, the craft of building ship, not just overhauling them, had begun.[51]

As the lowcountry shipbuilding industry began to evolve, so too did the colonists' awareness of shipping legalities and loopholes that may have influenced their preferences in boat and ship design. In 1687, a South Carolina statute provided for a bond for settlers to have vessels built in the colony. This law was in accord with Acts of Trade then in force. The Assembly's drive for economic diversity obviously extended to subsidizing the shipbuilding industry. There was evidently a need for a different type of vessel designed to meet the requirements of the shallow waters of the colony. Edward Randolph wrote from Charleston requesting "another vessel—that draws much less water" than the swift boat he had lost in Virginia. He stressed that he needed "an able coaster well acquainted with the flats and sands up the shoars from this place [Carolina]."[52]

Enforcement of navigation regulations may have influenced new boat designs, as shipbuilders tried to create boats designed to evade restrictive colonial laws. As early as 1696 a clause in the Act of Trade dealt with boat registration in the colonies. It required all those trading with the American colonies to register their vessels. In addition, a declaration under oath was required stating that the boats were completely owned by British subjects and not in partnership with a co-owner from another nation if the owner was to avoid certain specified duties and bonds. This was a tradition that continued through the Revolution. Before embarking on a voyage, a ship was required to pay a bond guaranteeing that if certain enumerated goods were loaded at any port, they would be brought to England or an English port and not to a port of another nation. The anticipated outcome was that any ship owner or captain who did not go to an English port would be prosecuted and would usually lose the bond. The English government believed that channeling all trade through English ports and thereby receiving income from duties and taxes would benefit the Crown, that English merchants would benefit from having a monopoly on sales, and that this would facilitate increased prices in the colonies. Colonial traders would be financially penalized for trading with foreign countries. Registration was thus a means of requiring the master of any boat arriving in an American port from Europe or from another colony to show a certificate of registration as a license to trade without having to pay a bond or duty. The act put the burden of regulating illegal traffic upon officials at colonial ports of entry. It also meant that if a boat entered without showing the royal collector of customs evidence of a valid registration, the governor and the naval officer were obliged to proceed against the boat's owner in vice admiralty court. With a view to preventing conspiracies and collaborations among customs officers participating in illegal trade transactions, the government entrusted the administration of the clause to two separate officials. For example, both the naval officer and the collector made records of manifests, entries, and registers of ships trading in their ports. The same principle was applied to the registration of vessels: the collector and the governor (or his naval officer) administered the oath jointly, and both endorsed the ship's certificate. Consequently, both collectors and governors kept records of registers issued.[53]

One of the most common problems with the registration record was that the proportion of shares held by each owner was not listed. This makes it impossible to assess a merchant's economic interest in the fleet without reference to other paperwork such as bills of sale, partnerships, and other records. It is equally difficult to identify the home fleet with certainty. A vessel might have only a slight connection with the port at which it was registered, for example. A boat managed by a merchant or planter in Rhode Island would be re-registered in Charleston if a share in it was purchased there. This might take place before the ship made a second voyage to Nassau, Bahamas, so that a Rhode Island boat would then be officially registered in Charleston. In a similar fashion, a merchant residing in Charleston could buy a major share in a vessel before it left New York, using his agent there to swear out a new register. Even if the vessel was operated by its Charleston owner, it could continue to sail on a New York certificate until there was a change in ownership. Without *any* registration, a boat was thus considered a foreign vessel and subject to different fees and restrictions. The names of small boats owned by planters (sometimes claiming the planter as master, with slave patroons or captains) do appear in the record of registers.

But the compilation of any statistics from the ship registers is severely compromised because "intercolonial" boats engaged in shipping goods within one colony were not required to carry registers as were the ships and boats trading with the West Indies, Europe, and Africa. In South Carolina, the Atlantic and intercolonial trade was almost exclusively restricted to Georgetown, Beaufort, and Charleston. It was usual for merchants at these southern ports to bring their staple products from plantations and to consign their goods upriver. The local river market was therefore very busy. Activities of the boats engaged in this thriving local trade must be reconstructed from other sources, notably wills, inventories of estates, and bills of sale, not from shipping registers.[54] There was one very strategic loophole in the registration requirement that gave the merchants and planters further trading freedom. The registration clause applied only to "decked" oceangoing or coastal vessels and not to "undecked" boats doing business within plantation waters. Technically, officials considered decked vessels to be oceangoing ships capable of carrying on illegal trade with the foreign West Indies. These vessels, however, were built for the inland waterways of the Charleston area, and because they carried rice a protective boat deck was preferred. They did not have the crew quarters or storage space to store the provisions adequate for long voyages, and Charleston's customs officers treated them as coasters. These boats included a variety of sloops, shallops, lighters, moses boats, flatboats, periaguas, wherries, and canoes. Instead of registration, the numerous inland and coastal boats were required to hold permits for the local trade so crucial to plantation economy. These were administered by naval officers of the locality and made the boats' owners exempt from taking out bonds.[55] Permits had to be purchased by the boat owner and had to list the owner and boat captain.

Decked vessels were required to clear each voyage with customs officials imposing an impossible requirement on plantation owners. This administrative obstacle may have led to a proliferation of undecked or semidecked vessels and an increased use of dugout canoes or variations on them in the Carolina colony.[56] Registration records also provide information about larger shipbuilding and ownership. Increases in these spheres reflect the growing strength and diversity of the local economy and provide details about the types of vessels built in the lowcountry. The largest vessel owned locally was fifty tons burthern, two others were forty tons, and several more thirty tons or less. It is possible to conclude that a small but continually active shipbuilding industry existed by the end of the seventeenth century.[57]

Trends that had an effect on the character and significance of the colony's boat culture throughout the colonial period emerged as early as the first decades of settlement. It is evident that Native Americans and Africans with boating skills were a vital part of this adaptation in the inland riparian and shoreline waters. Specifically, the canoe hull, a form linked to these two groups, became one of the most enduring boat designs in South Carolina. European immigrants brought a variety of seventeenth-century boats with hull shapes and sail designs typical of those used contemporarily in France, England, and the northern colonies. Other designs were modified to reflect the influence of the West Indies. New designs were required by the settlers to suit the needs of a different kind of environment, but they were also influenced by early devious attempts to short-circuit the Navigation Acts. At the same time, settlers were still dependent on boats registered, owned and built in the Caribbean or in England. Neither Europeans nor Africans arrived in the colony with culturally

Figure 3. Russell seagoing canoe. Courtesy of SCIAA.

pristine ideas about boats and boatbuilding. Both groups encountered and probably influenced each other in colonial settings, having served as boat crew, aboard ships, or in shipyards in Africa and the West Indies prior to their arrival in Carolina.[58] Thus, the maritime economic center of the colony was Charleston, where a variety of vernacular boatbuilding cultures, some of which initially may have been fairly distinctive, meshed and intertwined further as the communities grappled with the challenge of exploiting a new landscape.

Early Watercraft and the Longevity of the Canoe Design: The Archaeological Record

Africans, Native Americans, and Europeans built and used small single-log canoes from prehistoric times to the mid-twentieth century. The South Carolina State database lists a total of nineteen canoes located underwater in local rivers, including the east and the west branches of the Cooper, Edisto, Waccamaw, Wateree, and Combahee Rivers. The State recorded a number of canoes reported as either underwater or protruding from of river banks; these are usually named after the finder or the location, such as the Ferguson canoe, the Kizer

Judy canoe, the Cut Dam canoe, and the Chessey Creek canoe. Archaeologists took drew, photographed, and described these boats, leaving them in situ.[59]

Examples of a variety of canoe types can be viewed by the public at locations such as the Santee Canal Park in Moncks Corner, Middleton Place in West Ashley, the South Carolina State Museum in Columbia, the Charleston Museum, and the Horry County Museum. Most canoes in museum collections are associated with plantation usage in the eighteenth and nineteenth centuries.[60] In 1977 South Carolina archaeologists recovered a semicomplete cypress canoe, still attached to its tree trunk, from the Waccamaw riverbank. Although it was a dugout, it contained tool marks made by an adze and a saw, suggesting a later time period. The makers could have been Native American or African slaves, hired African American or Native American boat makers, or European Americans. Whoever made the canoe had access to metal or glass tools. The canoe was approximately fourteen feet seven inches long and two feet nine inches wide. A large crack runs along the length, and this was probably the reason the maker abandoned the project. The canoe, dubbed the "roots canoe," is currently displayed at the South Carolina State Museum in Columbia.[61]

Figure 4. Historic period canoe. Courtesy of SCIAA.

Only four reported canoes have been positively identified as built by Native American on the basis of carbon dating. Two prehistoric canoes discovered in the Hilton Head area and on Kiawah Island were dated by carbon-14 to 930+/–90 years B.C.E. and 740+/–200 B.C.E., respectively. Another canoe, recovered illegally from the Cooper River by a diver, was confiscated by the Department of Natural Resources Enforcement Division. It was dated to 3770+/–60 B.C.E. and is currently stored at the South Carolina Institute of Archaeology and Anthropology field office in Charleston.[62] A second early canoe was discovered by two recreational divers, Doug Boehme and George Pledger, in 1999 and still remains underwater in the east branch of the Cooper River. The carbon-14 test results put the date at 4120+/–60 years B.C.E., thus placing it in the Archaic period. There have been numerous vague reports in the past of prehistoric canoes having been found; however, most cannot be substantiated, and fewer still of the canoes in question can be visited today.[63]

2.

Traders, Scouts, and Ferrymen

"What Number of Ships or other Vessels are there belonging to the Province; and what Number of Seafaring Men? What number and what sorts of vessels are built there?" queried a report written to the Lord Proprietors on May 7, 1707.[1] The answer was that there were not more than ten or twelve ships belonging to the colony. Neither were there more than twenty seafaring men. Another report added that the vessels built in the colony were "small as most proper for our American Trade amongst ourselves, some built here, some the northern plantations purchased by the merchants here. Wee are come to no great matter to building here for want of persons who undertake it tho no country in the world is [as] plentifully supplyed with timber for the purpose and [so] well stored with convenient rivers."[2]

The Lord Proprietors were referring to South Carolina's abundant supply of live oak and southern pine, both ideal woods for shipbuilding. Additionally, the convenience of riparian shipyards situated at the waters' edge made it easy for shipwrights to launch new ships straight off the stocks. Neither did the vessels built in the colony have to be particularly large for the coastal and Caribbean trades. What the Proprietors began to learn was that Charleston, with its settlements situated along extensive waterways, was home to a new, less formal kind of boatbuilding culture that met many of the colonists' needs.

The queries to the Proprietors were focused on shipbuilding as a traditional trade executed by trained shipwrights. The budding cottage industry of multipurpose vernacular coastal and river craft was overlooked in an official survey such as this one. Seamen, likewise, were envisioned as Europeans with titles and training aboard a seagoing vessel. In reality, the colony was a cultural meeting ground for building technologies and the coastal and inland boating skills of the many ethnic groups that had settled in the area. It was an industry that often did not lend itself to formal analysis, as many unregistered watercraft were built on plantations by slaves or working-class servants, bought, borrowed, or stolen from Native Americans.

Throughout the eighteenth century the English government regularly attempted to keep track of how each of the colonies was developing. Officials formulated questionnaires like the one quoted to garner detailed information on the nature and direction of economic activities and the numbers and kinds of people inhabiting the colonies. At the time of the report, Carolina's population was quantified as "thirteen hundred and sixty freemen, nine hundred free women, sixty white servant men, seventeen white free children, eighteen hundred negro slave men, eleven hundred Negro women slaves, five hundred Indian men slaves, six hundred Indian woman slaves, four hundred and fifty Negro children, and two hundred Indian children."[3] The colony's population was growing, and colonial reporters clearly viewed it as a white, black, and red community with social stratifications ranging from freemen and freewomen to servants and slaves. Within the stratum of white freemen were some skilled craftsmen such as shipbuilders or men with seafaring backgrounds. However, there were but a handful of these seafarers and shipbuilders at the beginning of the eighteenth century.

The report also described the several Native American nations within a 150-mile radius of Charleston with whom the colonists could trade. Most of this trade was conducted by "English men who go upriver in pirryagues."[4] During the 1700s trade with Native Americans increased and European traders became familiar with the landscape, later venturing further inland. One prominent leader of the expanding Native American trade ventures was Landgrave Joseph Blake, who twice occupied the governorship, from 1694 to 1695 and again from 1696 to 1700. He personally invested in the so-called Indian trade and used all the political clout he could garner to support its expansion. British authorities established an Indian Commission with the task of regulating trade so that it would be more equitable for Native Americans, creating more profit for merchants, and securing greater safety for the province through relationships with these Native American communities. Clearly, balancing these goals was a challenge.[5]

Commissioners were generally assembly men with the most experience in Native American affairs. They were not supposed to engage in trade directly or indirectly when serving but often did. The main activity of members, as recorded in their journals, focused on abuses of Native Americans by unscrupulous traders. In an attempt to remedy these situations, commissioners required traders to secure licenses and bonds, which could be revoked as a control measure. Enforcing adherence to the licensing system was another problem in itself. The most demanding jobs of commissioners became hearing the complaints of Native

Americans. Even as the commissioners attempted to solve existing problems, increasing frontier expansion of trade caused new conflicts. One of the major causes of the Yamassee War in 1715 was the failure of Indian trade regulations to solve these problems.[6]

Native Americans frequently charged deerskin traders with committing thefts, engaging in brutality, and encouraging a huge debt for rum. Among the lists of grievances were accusations that traders seized boats under false pretenses. Forster, chief of the Tuscaroras, complained that a trader named Daniel Callihaun had taken a canoe from him, pretending that it had been sold to him for twenty shillings.

Essentially there were two groups of traders. One group was composed of wealthy planters, and the other was composed of merchants doubling as traders. This second group also functioned as the leaders of Charleston's political and colonial economic center, serving in the Commons House and on the Indian Trade Commission and appointing each other to various public offices. These traders included individuals like Ralph Izard, James Moore, Benjamin Motte, Samual Everleigh, Richard Beresford, and Captain Musgrave. Another group comprised small traders, often adventurers, without firm roots in a landed society. They worked for themselves initially but later, as trade monopolies developed, sought opportunities to work for more established trader-planters. After 1716, the colonial government regulated the public trading system.[7]

The dominant traders were inclined to blame lesser traders for the decline in trading relationships with Native Americans. Governor Moore, himself a trader, characterized small traders as "barbarous, heathenish, immoral, with an unjust way of living and dealing." Yet, wealthy traders, among them Henry Wigginton, were charged with employing unlicensed traders. The traders all escaped without a fine, and Wiggington was appointed to a seat on the Indian Trade Commission. Many other trader-planters also tolerated misbehaviors by small traders who worked for them.[8]

Charleston by this time was a prominent trading center of the colonial South. Deerskins were a most lucrative trade item, regularly arriving at the harbor export, and Native Americans were well aware of the economic value of this trade. In 1701, a disastrous incident involving the Sewee people demonstrated that there were clearly tensions deriving from the Sewees' doubts that they were benefiting fairly from this trade. When gentleman explorer John Lawson encountered a community of Sewee, they related a dramatic story about an attempt to undercut English traders, whom they regarded as "no better than cheats" in their business dealings. The Sewee, after consultation among their heads and without a single dissenting vote, agreed to find the English markets across the ocean. Boatbuilders in the community were employed in building the biggest and best canoes they were capable of producing. According to

Lawson, in his Euro-centric interpretation of events, this was the equivalent of the Sewee forming a "naval fleet." He described how "the affair was carried out with a great deal of secrecy and expedition, so in a small time they had gotten a navy, loading and provisions, and hands to set sail, leaving only the old, impotent and the minors at home 'till their successful return."[9] Some of this fleet of adventurers were reportedly lost in a storm at sea, while others were captured by English ships and taken as slaves. The attrition of men in the community left Sewee widows to wander over to the Wando, with whom they intermarried. By 1716, those remaining in the small Sewee community were taken as slaves by the French settlers living along the Santee River.[10]

Between 1699 and 1715 the average importation of deerskins by English merchants was estimated at 54,000 skins annually. Trade peaked in 1706, when 121,335 deerskins were shipped to England. The high desirability of this commodity led deerskin traders as far as a thousand miles into the North American interior. The traders stored dressed deerskins at "factories" or trading posts at the borders of Native American settlements. For travel overland the most popular type of transportation was packhorses, but traders also used wagons and, on occasion, Native American bearers.[11] Deerskins, each weighing between 150 and180 pounds, were kept at posts until enough had been accumulated to make up a boatload. The boats carrying these heavy loads were designed to go against currents of up to four knots under oar. Small boats and narrow hulls were best suited to this purpose.[12]

Drawings by Philip Georg Friedrich von Reck, who visited the southeast in the 1700s, provide a visual impression of these canoe-like craft piled high with cargo and moving upstream with only four oarsmen. The same sketch shows a beamier boat referred to as a "flat bateau," which was evidently having problems negotiating the tide and was being towed by a smaller boat. A sharp bow or prow was a critical feature; von Reck he commented on one of his sketches that "Mr. Carlson caused a flat bateau to be made so heavy and so unsuitable for the Savannah River . . . the prow is not sharp and stops the water."[13] Once the boats reached Charleston or Port Royal, slaves were involved in the trimming, weighing, and packaging of the skins for shipment. Robin, an African slave, earned four pounds per month for his owner working in a storehouse in Charleston in the spring of 1717.[14]

Africans and Native Americans were either contracted for a trip or hired from their owners as oarsmen for the trade boats. This suggests that there were not enough European traders to man these boats, that those who were available were not sufficiently proficient or experienced as oarsmen to maneuver boats in the strong river tides and currents, and that rowing was considered manual labor best suited to the enslaved and working classes. In 1716, one arrangement entailed a wage of nine pounds for six weeks' wages for the services of two slaves. Native Americans often received their pay in trade goods. Traders were instructed not to deal with any "white person" and not to "sell, truck, barter any Slave, Skins, Furs or other Things whatsoever, as you shall or may purchase from the Indians." At one Indian Trade Commission meeting, a local storekeeper was ordered to deliver to a "Westoe Indian" the outstanding payment of a striped "duffel blanket" and half a yard "strouds" for his services in rowing the canoe, loaded with goods, upriver and then returning according to his promise with the periauga loaded down with skins from a factory in the north. Often, the costs of hiring oarsmen were deducted from the gross profit of the trip.[15]

Colonial officials were caretakers of watercraft used for Indian trade and provided instruction about boating safety. Certain boats were considered public property. Captain Charles Glover was instructed to keep in good repair "all the Public Periagoes . . . that came within his View, Jurisdiction, or Employ," and Native Americans hired under contract as oarsmen for colonial traders were accompanied on board by a representative European. One letter mentions that traders feared the risks of sending a cargo of knives aboard trade vessels with hired Native American oarsmen, because "there were no irons aboard." The inherent risks of mutiny by oarsmen and of theft of tempting cargoes were a prevalent concern. Lists of instructions given to traders who supervised the boat crews reveal a range of problems experienced aboard these trading boats. These lists included the suggestion that small periaguas or canoes were better suited to negotiating the river currents than any other boats; that skins should be well secured on board and sheltered from rain and bad weather; and that crews should anchor the boats in the middle of the river at night and not go ashore. On a sterner note, they admonished the crews that no trader should fall asleep in the boat, embezzle rum, or blow himself up with gunpowder.[16]

In the first two decades of the 1700s, Native American and African oarsmen were also used aboard the canoe and periaugua guard and patrol boats used in conflicts and to obtain intelligence on the activities of other European powers, including Spain and France, during periods of international tensions aggravated by Queen Anne's War (1701–1714) and, a year later, by the Yamassee Uprising (1715). A boatman who was familiar with the waterways could navigate between the major inland rivers and even travel between Charleston and Florida without venturing into the open sea. The Inland Passage was also of benefit to marauding parties of Spaniards and Indians who could quietly slip into South Carolina in their canoes and raid plantations.[17]

Along the coastline and on the Sea Islands, detachments of soldiers manned lookouts in small clapboard huts or crudely built watchtowers. The role of the watch was to light a beacon, fire cannons, or carry messages by canoe to the local militia upon the approach of raiders. At the start of Queen Anne's War, in 1701, a lookout was placed at Daufuskie Island. In 1702, two more lookouts were established in Port Royal Sound, staffed with four Europeans and eight Native Americans. The House of Commons ordered that the militia should consider "what boats, Canoas, and Periaugers y' watches, in case of Allarams."[18] In 1703, when a Spanish invasion seemed imminent, the coastline watches were organized into a company. A captain, a lieutenant, and nineteen watchmen made up a watch team ordered to garrison the stockade forts and also to patrol the Inland Passage in three periaguas constructed of cedar.[19]

By 1707, scout watches no longer simply observed the waterways from a tower and a few guard boats but actively patrolled or scouted the Inland Passage in boats fitted out with sails and oars. An act passed in 1713 lists details about the boats used in coastal patrols and recommends that "there be with all possible expedition bought for the use of ye Public, six cyprus Periaugers, forty feet long, and five feet wide, att Least, with seventy eight pairs of oars to be kept, one in the North Edisto, two near the head of Stono River, and three near Charles Towne, for the carrying of men in case of an invasion."[20]

In 1733, a young man named Jonathan Bryan commanded the scout boat that patrolled the inland water passage around Port Royal. Later he became a wealthy planter in South Carolina and led a "voyage of Discovery and Observation" into Georgia in an oared boat with ten crew members. It was probably a periagua manned by slaves and former scouts. The conditions they endured and the lifestyle they adopted was probably very similar to those crews faced aboard a scout boat. Thus, he was well prepared to "endure all the Hardship of Wind and Weather, and not the least shelter," as they made their way, living off the land by fishing and hunting. His crew members, like the scouts, were "a hardy kind of Men, thoroughly acquainted with all the Water Passages and Row by Day and Night." Scouts could be compared to amphibious marines in their military role for the colony. They fought from their boats or on beaches and riverbanks. Their weapons included muskets, with paper-wrapped cartridges kept in a leather box, bayonets, cutlasses, or light hatchets. They wore either civilian clothing or possibly seamen's dress. Scouts were characterized as shiftless men who needed to be closely supervised. John Barnwell, a planter and engineer at Port Royal Sound, described them as "a Wild and Idle people and continually Sotting if they gett any Rum for Trust or money. Yet they are greatly useful . . . if Tenderly managed for as their chiefest Imploy is to hunt the Forest or Fish . . . so there is scarce one of them but understands the Hoe, the Axe, the Saw, as well as their Gun and Oar." Colonel Barnwell, like many other Englishmen, although skilled as an engineer and charged with building the fortifications along the colony's coastline, claimed that he was "little versed in working a schooner or another vessel." He was also reliant on the hardy scout's abilities as an outdoorsman to hunt, fish, and guide him "thro a very intricate passage among marshes with so many turnings and windings"[21]

A scout boat patrol, supervised by Captain Thomas Nairne and his patrolling crew, comprised four whites and six Yamassee Native Americans. Under the leadership of John Cochran, the crew was reduced to two whites and two Cusabo Native Americans, because the Yamassee were becoming increasingly hostile and were clearly a liability to colonial ventures. This small crew patrolled the vast distance of one hundred twenty miles between Port Royal and Spanish Florida. Colonial authorities also established a scout boat patrol under Captain Fenwick, which monitored the Stono River mouth and Port Royal. The scout boat, considered a militia galley, was essentially a canoe hull widened by sawing a long dugout in half and joining the two halves. It was square sterned and often longer, wider, and deeper than a canoe. There are detailed descriptions of the process that provide important and detailed insights into the design features and construction sequence followed in building a periagua. The building of a scout canoe began with a cypress or cedar log, hewn flat on two sides and sharpened at both ends. The outside of the log was shaped, and three holes, known as gauge holes (to gauge the amount of wood to scoop out), were drilled at intervals along the flattened bottom. In the next step of the process, builders flipped the log over and scooped out and hollowed the inside, using chopping tools, until the gauge holes were exposed. The sides of the canoes tapered in thickness from about three inches at the bottom to an inch and a half at the gunwales. Small framing members and thwarts (seats running across the beam) reinforced the thin hull. Sideboards, or strakes, were placed along the top of the gunwales. These served to increase the scout periagua's depth. A stem, a keel, and a sternpost were attached, and a rudder was fixed to the sternpost with iron straps and pintles. Finally, with the construction process completed, the hull was painted and decorated. Periaguas less than thirty feet in length apparently carried only one mast, while longer craft stepped two gaff-rigged masts. Sailing was an auxiliary means of propulsion, with oars as the main sources of movement. Some scout boats were as large as thirty-five feet with a beam of six feet, rowed by up to ten oarsmen and, in addition, sailed by two gaff-rigged masts.

Certain boats, such as whaleboats, a type of craft popular in colonial America, were also converted into or utilized as scout boats with extra rowing stations for the crew, often fitted with blunderbuses, or swivel guns. Additional boat accessories included a grapnel anchor, oars, tarpaulin, ropes, and water casks.[22] A whaleboat was a double-ended, plank-constructed longboat.[23] For example, whaleboats were converted into scout boats used by Colonel Barnwell for exploring, mapping, and sounding the creeks and coastline for military purposes. He concluded that the scout boat was more suitable than the other types of boats he had at his disposal. Pilot boats "by reason of drawing five feet of water were useless and unwieldy in wind . . . the perriaugoe was too long to go in a great sea," so instead he ordered a small scout boat.[24] James Oglethorpe of

Georgia was very impressed with the performance of these scout boat canoes, even presenting one to the Queen of England as a gift in 1735.[25]

Scout canoes were used not only for "giving intelligence to vessels" but also for capturing runaways. Anyone who captured a slave on land or in a boat on the sea coast, a mile within the shore, or within two miles of the coast received a reward of forty shillings. The Port Royal Scout boats were equipped with twenty-five pounds of gunpowder and seventy-five pounds of bullets. Chiefs appointed Native Americans to serve in the scout canoes, for which they were paid around fifteen pounds per annum. If they ran away during their time of duty and were subsequently captured, their employer, with the consent of the chief, could order moderate punishments.[26] Legislation passed in 1719 authorized trustworthy male slaves between sixteen and sixty years to provide service to the Carolina settlement in "time of alarms and for encouragement of sailors to serve the same against our enemies." Captains, lieutenants, and ensigns were charged with the joint responsibility of drawing up lists of "negroes, mulattoes, mustees, and Indian slaves" to serve as boat crews.[27]

Native American trade and coastal defense were stepping stones to successful international commerce. In addition to boats and boat crew, trade required depots for landing and loading cargoes along inland river systems and a system for ferrying goods across from one bank to another. An early report to the Lord Commissioners for Trade and Plantations described the problem of lack of local shipping that handicapped the colony's growth. Edward Randolph noted that "the Lord Proprietors have taken up vast tracts of land for ther own use as in Colleton County and other places where the land is most commodius for settlement which prevents them from peopling the place and makes them less capable of preserving themselves."[28]

Commodious or convenient land for settlement was land situated in proximity to a navigable waterway, thus enabling cargoes to be transported easily to the port of Charleston. The Lord Proprietors were well aware of the critical advantages of waterfront properties. "Wee are in designe to employ some able person for ye discovery and sounding all ye roads and rivers near ye and how far up ye rivers are navigable and with vessels of what burden," they wrote to the Commissioners.[29] Reprimands to Lord Carteret, one of the Proprietors, showed that the Commissioners were well aware of the value of waterfront real estate and the potential problem of personal monopolies. In a letter to Carteret, the Commissioners for Trade and Plantations wrote succinctly that "you are to consider a convenient place for a ferry upon every navigable river and pick a convenient place . . . to be set out 1000 acres which whosoever takes up shall be obliged to keep a ferry for ferrying over men and horses" and also noted that "any man that shall take up his hand in a creek navigable for boats onley shall have but a sixt part of his depth fronting to the said creek so ye more persons may come to have benefit of it."[30]

Advertisements for private land described the access to river navigation, highlighting again the value placed on waterfront property. A sale notice in an issue of the *South Carolina Gazette* from 1739 lists a plantation three and a half miles from Charleston that had "a Dwelling House and convenient Outhouses, with an extraordinary Pasture under fence, and navigable Creek leading to the Ashley River sufficient for the largest Pettiaugua at half tide."[31] Sales notices for tracts of land also noted the distance from a ferry landing; one such site sold by Hugh Ferguson was advertised as "containing 380 acres, joining on the North side of the Ashley River, three Miles above the Ferry."[32]

In the last decades of the seventeenth century, settlers had characterized Charlestown as "a fairly compact settlement of 500 to 600 people living along the Ashley River a few miles from the ocean"; these settlements evolved during the next century into ten political and religious divisions, called parishes. During this period the greatest influx of settlement occurred in St. Johns Parish on the Cooper River. By then, a definite pattern of socioeconomic patterns began to emerge. Anabaptists and French Protestants peopled Upper St. Johns, and English, Irish, and West Indies colonists settled in Lower St. Johns. The latter group was composed mainly of individuals who had secured their fortunes in England or in the West Indies prior to arriving in the colony. They were the elite, and they sought to improve upon their economic status rather than to achieve a new status.[33]

Lower St. Johns, on the banks of the Cooper River, featured some of the best land in the province. More than 59 percent of its residents owned one thousand acres or more each. This was 38 percent more land per individual than was found in any other settlement on Cooper River. Intermarriage among the families of these elite landowners served to consolidate their wealth and keep it within social confines of Lower St. Johns parish. As planters and businessmen, this elite became an integral part of the fabric of Charleston's social, political, and business community. As stockholders in merchant firms, political officers, and primary investors in shipbuilding enterprises, they were generally recognized as economically and politically dominant and often ruthless figures in the colonial community.[34]

In decades prior to 1720, St. Johns parish practiced a diverse economy of deerskin trade, livestock raising, and naval stores production. The center of all this economic activity was the town of Childesbury. To promote the economic prosperity of the region, these wealthy planters collectively submitted petitions to the General Assembly for a communal fair, a market, public buildings, and, most important, a ferry landing. At that time, Childesbury was a frontier town, and an intricate system of overland and river transportation linked inland settlers to the economic center at Charleston.[35] Strawberry ferry landing, as it came to be known, was the key element in making the inland plantations economically viable at a time when there were few bridges and roads were in poor condition. The colonists also built another landing, known as Ashley ferry, in St. Andrews parish on the Ashley River in 1711.[36]

Several towns established during the early 1700s failed to achieve long-lasting viability through the eighteenth and nineteenth centuries. The two that achieved economic sustainability had ferry landings. According to James Childe's 1707 plat map and 1718 will, the town of Childesbury consisted of 185 numbered lots, two town squares, and a market area. Over time the town acquired full-time residents, including a doctor, a lawyer, a shoemaker, and several tailors, butchers, tanners, and carpenters.[37] A 1724 map shows that the Ashley Ferry town contained 102 plots. Residents of the town included a blacksmith, a carpenter, and a vintner. The legislature passed an act in 1723 providing for public and open markets to be held in Ashley Town every Wednesday and Saturday. The South Carolina Assembly occasionally held sessions in the town, generally during times of epidemic or illness in Charleston.[38]

Although it is clear that colonists established ferry services, there is scant historical evidence of the construction of the actual ferry boats in these early years of ferry operations. One can speculate on the basis of later evidence. A flat boat, or barge design, was probably most suitable. The *South Carolina Gazette* advertised for sale "a new large flat boat such as for a ferry" at Pon Pon on the Edisto River. These vessels were basically flat, rectangular platforms of shallow draft and minimal freeboard, propelled by hand or tide and designed to operate in the relatively calmer waters of South Carolina's rivers and sounds. Ferry boat slips at landings provided a shallow gradient upon which the boat could drop a loading ramp to allow passengers, livestock, and wheeled vehicles such as carriages to board. In calm shallow water, ferrymen poled the boat and its cargo across the river. In deeper water, a rope was stretched across the river and the crew pulled the boat along.[39]

Ferry companies or people who owned the adjacent waterfront property usually had other supporting business endeavors on either side of the ferry landing. This land usage was associated with developments such as wharves, stables, plantations, and taverns. In some instances, companies also operated stagecoaches that traveled between taverns. By 1744 the Commissioners of Trade and Plantations barred the establishment of privately owned ferries within a mile of a public ferry. At this time the legislature became more involved in regulating public ferries, setting up a licensing system and establishing fees and ferry slip maintenance standards.[40]

Waterscapes and Boat Landings: The Archaeological Record

At the turn of the century, linkages of rivers and creeks from inland depots to the Charleston seaport were vibrant frontier settings of social change, growth, and population dispersal from the Old World to the New. Along the waterways, settlers struggled to meet the challenge of transportation in their new environment and addressed early problems of moving people and produce along river networks by building a variety of causeways across marshes and adding wharves where vessels could dock.[41]

South Carolina archaeologists have investigated several of these docks at former plantations, shipyards, and ferry landings. They have compared technological attributes, noting that the most common construction method was to fill a log crib box and sink it onto the riverbed. Causeways were landings extending into rivers and consisted of soil, shell, gravel, and brick rubble. Associated fill artifacts included liquor bottles, coins, bricks, ballast stones, jewelry, smoking pipes, ceramics, and other domestic items, conveniently allowing archaeologists to create broad temporal categories—colonial, antebellum, and postbellum—during which certain designs may have been used in construction.[42]

3.

Immigrant Shipwrights and Shipyard Slaves

In 1752 a Scottish shipwright, James Stewart, wrote to his father, John Stewart, from Charleston.[1] "We came in here with about 600 pounds Sterling, we put on our treusers went to work by the day & raised Slaves by degrees lived snug & untill of late nobody knew what we were worth, and now we have got Experience & are known and Respected by the first Rank & wear Silk Jackets and Ruffels."[2] He went on to say that he had eaten the "bread of servitude" and the "bread of foreigners" but now felt he had enough experiences in his life since leaving London not only to understand people from different classes and cultures but also to be a good businessman and "to know the value of Money." The Charleston shipbuilding industry allowed many shipwrights to rise from poverty to a status of relative esteem and wealth unattainable in their home country. Stewart noted that Carolinians equated wealth with the number of slaves a man owned and that if he and his business partner, John Ross (sometimes given as Rose) who together operated shipyard on Hobcaw Creek, had a dozen "negroes," they would never need to work again.[3] He quoted a local doctor who said that "he who has the most Slaves has the greatest chance of being engaged by captains" who brought their vessels to Charleston for repairs and maintenance. Shipwrights hired slave carpenters and patroons from plantations until they had sufficient income to purchase their own shipyard slaves and train them in the art of shipbuilding.

Use of slaves in urban shipyards and as offshore labor had its roots in this period of the 1750s. These maritime labor assignments were linked to an era of greater independence and new values for Africans. Ship artwork by people of African heritage in the Bahamas suggests that, despite their low economic status, African Bahamians were familiar with ship construction and rigging.[4] By the time of the Revolution, shipbuilding was one of the "most lucrative mechanic industries" in Charleston. The 1740s to the 1760s heralded the commencement of an era of unprecedented shipbuilding growth in South Carolina. Public fears about slave uprisings limited agricultural expansion, and the capital that would have been tied up in slave purchasing instead was diverted to activities like shipbuilding.[5] King George's War (1744–1748) brought about losses on the high seas and drove up the value of boats, making the ownership of colonial shipyards more attractive, as French and Spanish privateers targeted not only large, fully laden warships but also "small pettiaguas drove on Shoar & plundered, our Coast being left without any defense," as the influential planter Henry Laurens complained in a letter to a Boston merchant, Thomas Savage.[6]

Rice prices were increasingly unstable and fell dramatically, causing merchants to explore new opportunities as shippers, generating the need for the construction of more ships.[7] In addition, the quality of lumber and of the workmanship evident ships built in the colony, both of which had previously been in doubt outside the colony, were promoted by high-ranking officials as equal to the English merchant vessels. "We have in plenty a sort of wood called the live oak for timbers which seem admirably adapted to that use," wrote Governor James Glen to the Board of Trade in 1751. He elaborated: "Builders prefer it even to the best Oak that can be met with in the yards of England and we have great quantities of yellow pine for planking, nor are we in want of plenty of Masts and Naval Stores."[8]

The British Navy Board gave extremely favorable inspection reports on American shipyard work. Timber suitable for building ships was readily available in the southern colonies at a time when resources were dwindling in Europe. A lack of timber for building ships was a threat to England's sea power. On the more practical side, why exhaust precious English oak or bring timber from thousands of miles away when shipwrights could use local timber to build a ship in the colonies and then the completed vessel could be sailed back to England ready for service? Rather than purchase ships built by competing European nations, authorities argued, it was better to utilize Britain's colonial possessions, especially those with good sources of timber like South Carolina and Georgia, as shipbuilding centers.[9]

Between the Revolution and the Civil War, thousands of men were sent to the South from northern colonies and states to work all winter long in the live oak hummocks to supply timber to build the ships seen in ports around the world. Neither loggers nor skilled craftsmen, these men called themselves live oakers. Their laborious efforts included locating timber stands, obtaining cutting rights, and transporting oxen, timber carts, and provisions for five- to six-month periods. They had scant rations and, like slaves in the rice fields, survived the perils of malaria and venomous snakes, in the quest to target this ideal wood.[10] Property owners in South Carolina during the eighteenth century frequently advertised land for sale by calling attention its stands of live oak. In advertisements in the *South Carolina Gazette,* ships' live oak and pine construction was often used as part of a sales pitch to indicate the quality of construction. On May 24, 1754, a sale notice for a schooner that would carry between ninety-five and a hundred barrels of rice noted that the vessel was "extraordinary well-built, live oak and red cedar timber, with two streaks of white oak plank under her bends, the rest yellow pine." Another equally popular but less abundant wood source was cedar. It was favored especially for its ability to resist the tenacious and destructive teredo (*Teredo navalis*) shipworms.[11] Both Carolina live oak and cedar apparently increased the life expectancy of ships. In general, a wooden boat lasted fifteen years.[12] Carolina-built ships, however, were known to have a life span of twenty to thirty years.[13] The *Queenly,* built in South Carolina in 1739, sailed for twenty-seven years trading between South Carolina and Georgia. When the fifteen-ton schooner *Friendship* was registered for trade in 1773, it was already twenty-eight years old, having been built in 1745 in Charleston.[14] In 1773 a story in the *South Carolina Gazette* described the 125-ton ship *Live Oak,* which "was constantly employed between this port and Europe" and which had been built on James Island, near Charleston, twenty-four years earlier.

Shipbuilders in the Charleston area were scattered around the peninsula. Areas with plots of land belonging to colonial shipwrights are listed in deeds, warrants, and newspaper notices at present-day locations including James Island, Johns Island, Dewees Island, and Mount Pleasant and on the East Branch of the Cooper River. The shipyards were generally situated close to water, and the sites were probably selected with the idea of "convenience," including proximity to timber sources and the presence of sufficient tidal ranges and depths to launch and bring ships into the yard and of mud flats, sand bars, or riverbanks to facilitate careening a vessel for repairs. These criteria may have varied in importance depending on the size of the vessels being built in the particular yard and on whether the yard served primarily to do maintenance and repair work or to actually build ships, although it is likely that many did both.[15]

There were clearly financial incentives for Stewart to make the journey to South Carolina and start a new life in the colony.[16] Shipbuilders like James Stewart, who came to the colonies as laborers, had previously been employed at large shipyards in England. As Scotsmen, these shipwrights often endured marginal working conditions and strenuous labor, even in the king's shipyard at Woolwich. When Stewart was a shipwright in training at this prestigious yard, he wrote to his father describing his living and working conditions. He asked for "a wig to worke in," as his was in very poor condition and "a strange horse hair one they made for me they being very dear here." Working in an exposed yard in very hot weather caused "scorching" of the skin and made his shortsighted eyes tender. His shoes were worn out, "since they are planking a 90-gun ship where we kiln the plank in hot wet sand over a large furnace where we go in to shovel on & off the sand which is sometimes so hot that we stay in 5 minutes." He also complained, with increasing irritation in his tone, that his family never wrote back and that he was in need of money and clothes. Eventually, his father sent him four guineas to pay for instruction in drafting as part of his training as a skilled shipwright, and some of his shipyard manual duties were reduced.[17]

When Stewart completed his training, he started making inquiries about joining his uncle Mungo Murray as his partner serving as a carpenter on ships around Europe. He explored several options, including entering into the service of the king of Sweden. But Swedes, he complained once again, were simply "malicious" and "deceitful." Journeys by boat were not to his liking either, because the long voyages were "worse than imprisonment . . . & if inflicted as a punishment for prisoners should be a very bad one." Even after some satisfactory voyages working as a ship's carpenter, a more lucrative employ, he was not content. "I do not find Contentment & Satisfaction in a Seafaring Life as in a Land One," he wrote, "and financial gain is not everything." By 1746, he began exploring possibilities of going to South Carolina, where "his Broyr in Law Capn White has a great deal of Intrest." Eventually, by July 1749, he engaged in articles to head to South Carolina to work as an apprentice to his uncle, Mungo Murray, who by now was a respected colonial shipwright.[18]

After settling in Charleston, Stewart wrote a letter to his father announcing: "[Arrived 13th after] a long and tedious passage, I can say but little of this country yet I am told my business is one of the best in ye province by the merchants here who are 2/3 Scots." His letter proceeds to detail the problems he and his uncle were having setting up a home. Over time they acquired their own shipyard slaves, and Stewart referred to their household and business partnership several times in his correspondence as a "family" of ten—seven slaves, one white servant, and two bachelors, John Rose and himself. Stewart seemed very satisfied with this new arrangement. They began to settle into their new domestic life, acquiring basic material goods as they had arrived with no household goods except their sea beds and some kitchen utensils. Stewart referred to their spartan downtown accommodations as "Bachelors Hall" and looked forward to having their nest "well feathered."[19]

Slaves are mentioned throughout his correspondence, reflecting either his changing economic status or his desire to own more workers. He states in a letter: "I have not had a shirt or stocking mended in this province but give them always to the Nigroes [*sic*] when tore or holes." He declares that to take on a hired African shipbuilding apprentice would require twenty or thirty guineas.

The better alternative, it seemed to him, was to hire slaves and to buy more to add to his existing seven as soon as the money became available.[20]

Like new colonist planters, shipwrights came to seek their fortunes. An eager welcome awaited immigrants who were craftsmen. There was a definite aura of superiority attached to artisans with European training. Most who came to the colonies recognized this appeal and exploited it to the full extent in the colonial press. Stewart established himself in the community with his uncle's help and formed a partnership with another Scottish shipwright, John Ross or Rose. Their first house, located in the city of Charleston, was destroyed by a hurricane. Stewart wrote, in a letter dated August 15, 1752, that they were in the process of building a new house on land outside Charleston where they had a twelve-year lease; he wrote that the site was "where the Kings Worke is done & 6 miles from toun in a healthy situation & Convenient for Shipbuilding."[21] This was evidently Hobcaw Point.

Shipbuilding activities flourished into the early eighteenth century around Hobcaw Plantation on the Wando River. The attractions of this location for shipbuilders included the depth of water in the river, the existence of a fresh water spring close to the shore, and its separation from the distractions of the city, which lured workers' attention from their tasks of building and maintaining vessels. A series of shipwrights had owned this shipyard prior to the Rose and Stewart partnership. The first owner was George Dearsley in the early 1700s. His widow married Thomas Bolton, who took over the operation. By the time he sold it to James Stewart and his partner, John Rose, in 1752, it was an established shipbuilding facility "for Kings Worke" outside Charleston.

The new owners' business acumen and success are evident from the sale of the shipyard by John Rose to William Begbie and Daniel Manson in 1769, after which John Rose was able to retire with a fortune of £30,000 sterling to his name. An advertisement in the *South Carolina Gazette* on November 30, 1769, by these new partners lists the services offered by the Hobcaw yard and by John Rose's other yard, Rose's Wharf in Charleston, including shipbuilding, heaving down, repairing, graving, and mast building. Apart from its service as a shipbuilding depot, the yard also represented a sales depot that supplied the products required for shipbuilding and repair, including live oak, cypress, and spars for topmasts, yards, and booms.[22]

The business partnership between these two men is typical of the network of Scottish patronage so prevalent in the colonial Atlantic world. Rose's family influence and connections to Stewart's uncle and benefactor in Charleston, Mungo Murray, provided the foundation for Stewart's apprenticeship and partnership. The London correspondent for the family, George Ouchterlony, reported about the early stages of the partnership to John's father, James Rose: "He [John Rose] & Mr. Stewart goe partners together in everything &

indentures are drawing up to that purpose."[23] The Rose family loaned the two men £120 in the form of a bond and, more important, provided twenty letters of introduction to influential merchants in Charleston.[24]

The two partners continued to request capital from the Rose network up until 1754. Correspondence reveals that although they believed they faced no real competition in Charleston from other shipbuilders, they had difficulty paying for labor and materials to keep up with the demand. The correspondences make it clear that they needed to own rather than hire slaves to make their business thrive. They also had to rely on the skills of other Charleston tradesmen, especially with their naval contracts. Another complaint, prior to their acquisition of Hobcaw, was that they simply did not have the space or specialized facilities to service ships adequately.[25]

Over time they used the Rose family loans to expand their wharf facilities and to purchase more slaves and train them in shipyard skills, eliminating the need for outside skilled labor. In October 1754, John Rose married his neighbor's daughter, Hester Bond, who was from a family considered to be Charleston gentry. In the colonial world this would be perceived as sensible choice, but clearly, she was not highly regarded by the Rose/Irvine family and was considered a drain on the shipyard resources and even a source of trouble in the relationship between the two partners—despite Stewart's earlier comment in 1751 that he wanted his partner to "get him a wife to take care of the House."[26] Bond's father was a successful planter who owned around a hundred slaves on land near Rose's on Hobcaw Point. He had also been a member of South Carolina legislature for some years. Clients admired and respected Rose, who was described as "an Honest sensible man" and as a "*great great* Ship Wright who came in recommended to me with a Broad Ax on his Shoulder in the year 1749."[27]

Scottish benefactors also had high hopes for Rose, describing him as diligent about his business, as well as prudent and frugal. Correspondence between his family members claims that Rose "turns out well & applys himself close to his business."[28] The small tensions that marked the relationship between Stewart and Rose early in the partnership seemed to escalate with Rose's marriage to Hester and his growing family. In 1751, when Rose secured his first loan from Europe, Stewart objected to signing the promissory note until Rose applied pressure, explaining that the shipyard simply would not succeed as a business enterprise with a start-up loan from relatives. By November 1755, writing after Stewart's death, George Ouchterlony commented negatively on the relationship between the two partners and found Stewart's disposition "to be of a stiff, dogged Temper which makes me less surprised that there was no right agreement with regard to Mr. Stewart's Estate." The London correspondent was referring to an ongoing disagreement between Rose and Stewart over how to divide their partnership assets. Correspondence indicates that Stewart, unknown to Rose, had inquired about placing lands in a "joynt Tennacy" ensuring absolute rights to the surviving partner, thereby excluding the deceased partner's heirs! Then, on June 24, 1755, James Stewart "was found dead in the woods with his gun by him with a string to the treegar & Round his foot" Rose could not account for his death, claiming it was a suicide and that "he shot himself and I believe there is none upon earth cann act. for it."[29]

The coroner's inquest yielded an official verdict of lunacy as the cause of Stewart's death. According to Rose, Stewart had drunk a lot and had recently taken to carrying a gun around. Rose claimed he was surprised to discover Stewart's intentions concerning the partners' assets, for he had always thought Stewart an honest man. He recounted information about Stewart's recent secret visits to lawyers and conversation with friends about the issue of their joint assets only after Stewart's death. This was troubling, and Rose believed he was certainly justified in acting in a similar vein toward Stewart's family after the suicide. He defensively argued that it "could hardly be criminal" and that he could cut off Stewart's family heirs in Scotland. The announcement of the so-called melancholy affair of Stewart is addressed in the same letter to his uncle as his plans for the shipyard assets and the news of the premature birth of his twin sons, named after his father, James, and his uncle, Charles Irvine.

This action caused consternation among relatives, including Stewart's uncle, Mungo Murray, who had assisted John Rose in early years, and their other relatives in Scotland.[30] There surely must have been speculation among the locals and among the relatives about the possibility that Rose had played a role in his partner's death. Regardless of the family turmoil John Rose caused, in later years he ultimately succeeded in Charleston society. He took 170 slaves with him to Jamaica when he left Charleston in 1782. In time, he became increasingly less interested in shipbuilding despite the high demand for his services, shifting his priorities toward the more prestigious activity of developing plantations with the entire Hobcaw fortune then at his personal disposal. It is estimated that between 1770 and 1772 Rose purchased 9,265 acres and a total of 221 slaves.[31]

Under the management of John Rose, Hobcaw shipwrights and their apprenticing slaves built and launched an impressive list of vessels from Charleston's shore. Two such ships were, in 1770, the *Magna Carta* of three hundred tons and the *New Carolina Packet,* intended for the London trade, the very next year. Names of other Hobcaw ships reflect the growing patriotic colonial sentiment: the *Liberty,* the *Fair American,* and the *Oliver Cromwell.* In 1778, along with many other shipwrights with Loyalist leanings, he was forced to sell out to Paul Pritchard, an Irishman from Belfast.[32] At the same time that James Stewart was investigating the possibility of emigrating to South Carolina as a shipwright, so were some of the elite Anglo-Irish Protestants like the Pritchards, a family of shipwrights. Although they had wealth and status in Ireland, they found England's control of the country irksome and a source of great uneasiness. As England's merchants devoured all the best commercial activity, the primary concern for shipbuilding families was that Ireland's abundant live oak, a vital resource, was being plundered for use in English shipyards. This raised concerns about the stability of their business in the long run. The exciting lure and challenge of a new beginning in a colony like South Carolina, more removed from English control, was great. Due to transportation problems in leaving Ireland, it was only in the early 1760s that the three brothers—Paul, William, and George Pritchard—arrived in Charleston.[33]

Overall, King George's War was politically and economically disruptive to Charleston's economy, but the peace years between 1748 and 1755 were a time of rapid recovery and even prosperity for some. The slave trade especially was established on a large scale, as the number of slaves brought into the province grew from 72 slaves in 1749 to 831 in 1751 and to more than 1,000 in 1752.[34] In the colonies, especially South Carolina, shipwrights found slaves to be a more permanent, cheaper, and therefore more attractive labor force, one based on tradition. The earlier tenants on Hobcaw, the Dearsley family, acquired seven slaves "by name old Dick, Ceesar, Charles, Roger, Nanny, Judith & Mary now resident at said plantation."[35] Slaves' names are listed in the property transactions between father and son. James Stewart also took every possible advantage of slave labor, constantly desiring to buy more slaves and to increase their training in the art of shipbuilding and their value. Paul Pritchard, who operated the yard during the Revolution, also relied heavily on shipyard slave labor. The nine slaves who helped him build and repair ships at Hobcaw are mentioned by name in his will: "the following Negroes . . . Portius, Sam Moosa, Henry Junk, Caesar, Little David, Big David, Cyrus, Passage and Gray, ship Carpenters and Caulkers, Stafford and George, Blacksmith's; my wenches Sue, Phyllis, and Chloe and my two house carpenters Sam and George."[36]

Planters and merchants requesting the service of shipyards, like that at Hobcaw, often had distinctive views about the quality of work and convenience of the facility. As a planter who owned vessels and engaged in the transatlantic trade, Henry Laurens represented the expectations and perceptions of a successful lowcountry colonist.[37] He believed that inland areas most suited to shipbuilding were those at the water's edge in proximity to abundant sources of live oak, pine, and cedar. Furthermore, there should be sufficient depth of water "that Vessels may ride with great safety and very little danger in Hurricane seasons." Preferably the oak should grow "upon the Sea Side" rather than on fresh water. By this, he probably meant that it should grow in the tidal zone of rivers alongside brackish water.[38] While supporting the notion of shipbuilding in South Carolina, Laurens reveals through his correspondence that the quality of shipbuilders' workmanship varied depending on how carefully a shipwright was selected for the job. It was, he proclaimed, "not a trifling business" for a ship to be designed and built for one's "own particular Trade and Exactly agreeable to a Draught."[39] He personally was interested in hiring the best available shipwright to do his work, even if it meant paying more per ton than the common rate, which was six pounds sterling per ton. He believed that employing shipwrights of integrity and competence to design South Carolina vessels would also give American-built vessels a better reputation and that South Carolina ships "would acquire the Character & Credit which they truly merit." He alluded to instances in which American-built ships had been downgraded and stereotyped by English shipwrights although the complaints referred to ships built in New England and Philadelphia, not South Carolina.[40]

While discussing the cost of shipbuilding in South Carolina with William Fisher, a Philadelphia ship owner, Laurens noted that "the Difference in the Cost of our Carolina-built Vessels is not the great objection to building here. That is made up in the different qualities of the vessels when built or some people think so." As land was cheap and work plentiful, the colonial shipwright had greater opportunities to obtain his own yard than a builder in England.

A shipyard required the skills of an assortment of tradesmen who were supervised by a master shipwright. Master shipwrights who came to the colonies were trained in both government or "royal" and private shipyards of Great Britain. Other shipwrights were scattered throughout the coastal villages, producing mostly small craft for coastal trade. Many traveled from one yard to the next in search of employment, which was haphazard. As a result, they gained experience in several yards and could often build both merchant vessels and warships. Few shipwrights became wealthy, although shipbuilding was a family trade and occasionally a family produced two or three generations of shipwrights. Other shipyard workers included joiners, who undertook tasks such as smoothing the outer planking, building rails on the upper decks, and finishing cabins; caulkers, who filled seams; and painters, plumbers, carvers, glaziers, and coopers, who put the finishing touches on the newly constructed vessel.[41]

It took almost a year in ordinary conditions to build a ship in colonial yards. Every operation required backbreaking labor by the shipwrights with whipsaw, broadaxe, adze, pod, plane, and chisel. Constructing the hull and launching the vessel were only the initial part of the operation. The masts still had to be stepped, spars, rigging, and running gear installed, and the sails fitted. These tasks, termed "finishing," had to be completed before the ship could take on provisions and a cargo for her first voyage. In a very real sense, building was a community enterprise with many specialized tasks.[42]

A Shipyard Setting: The Archaeological Record

The shipyard site (38CH1049) owned by Rose and Stewart is located along Hobcaw Creek in Mount Pleasant, South Carolina. It was placed on the National Register of Historic Places (NRHP) in 1974.[43] In 1989, during construction of a private dock along the foreshore of the Hernandez family property, the Underwater Archaeology Division of the South Carolina Institute of Archaeology and Anthropology (SCIAA) at the University of South Carolina conducted a reconnaissance survey that confirmed the presence of eighteenth- and nineteenth-century materials. These included "ballast rock, brick and ship frames eroding out of the bank, and two distinct areas on the foreshore containing wood cribbing and pilings—the remains of two of the three slipways and a wharf."[44]

Removal of a live oak to make way for the construction of the Hernandez's five-thousand-square-foot home uncovered the remains of a brick structure entangled in the tree's roots. This area was the focus of SCIAA's intensive archaeological investigations during the summer of 1993. The structure consisted of "of the lower remains of three brick walls forming an approximately seven-meter square enclosure. Only the south wall remains to its 7.35-meter length. While the west wall extends 6.9 meters to the north, the east wall has been all but destroyed, with only the southernmost 2 meters of structure remaining. A large live oak root had deflected along the inside of the once extant east wall, and most of the brick that once comprised this wall is absent. No evidence for a wall enclosing the north side of the structure was found."[45] Within the enclosure excavators recovered artifacts including numerous pipe stems (most dating from 1750 to 1800 or later), ceramics and glass (dating from the eighteenth and nineteenth centuries), iron and copper fasteners, wrought iron and brass fasteners, wound and drawn glass beads, gunflints marbles, buckles, thimbles, buttons, a horse's bit, a 1720 Dutch trade token, wine-glass stems, an adze, axe heads, a pair of dividers, a broken chain plate, and large amounts of burned faunal remains of pig, deer, bird, and fish.[46]

In 2004, in response to the pending subdivision of the Hernandez property, which contained a portion of the National Register site, the Office of Coastal Resource Management (OCRM) required intensive archaeological investigations in the proposed subdivision area. The State Historic Preservation Office (SHPO) consulted with OCRM and recommended that shovel testing excavations and perhaps test units be excavated to mitigate the impact to the site. Southern History and Archaeology Research (SEARCH) consultants used the original site grid established by SCIAA during the 1993 archaeological investigations.[47] The 2004 investigators, assisted by assorted young volunteers and anthropology and archaeology students from Trident Technical College and the

College of Charleston, encountered a potential clay floor with charcoal inclusions that was determined to be an industrial area (Feature 2) and a refuse midden or occupation area like a kitchen or tavern (Feature 3). Upon completion of their excavations, investigators attempted to integrate previous archaeological data generated by SCIAA in order to fully interpret their findings.

Historic plats and archaeological testing at Hobcaw provide insight about the landscape of a southern colonial yard. Typically, slave cabins on lowcountry plantations were located along the avenue of oaks terminating in the main or "big" house. This does not appear to be a spatial preference either at Pritchard's (as determined by SCIAA shovel testing) or at Fairbanks, another plantation/shipyard on the Wando River owned by Paul Pritchard in 1814. Historic plats and archaeological evidence revealed that, as at the Fairbanks shipyard, the slave quarters at Hobcaw were located to the right of the main house and slightly behind it. In addition to the slave quarters, the dwelling of a "resident worker manager" was also situated to the right of the main house and was associated with the densest cluster of kitchen rubble.[48] If Hobcaw Plantation followed this pattern, the worker and slave quarters would also have been the right of the main house, an area currently covered by a tar neighborhood road at the front entrance to Hernandez property.

A shipyard landscape may represent a working relationship between skilled slaves and whites different from that on plantations. In his correspondence with his father James Stewart repeatedly refers to his new Carolina "family" of ten persons, consisting of enslaved laborers who worked alongside free apprentices and shipyard owners, and the landscape should in turn reflect this increased fraternization. No historic shipyard plats, in the fashion of plantation plats, show the presence of slave cabins. They do show stables and a small house. Were the slaves housed with the white apprentices, or were their numbers so small that they were socially invisible to shipyard owners?[49] A 1786 plat shows the shipyard complex consisting of the main Pritchard shipwright house at the north end of an avenue of oak trees leading to the down to the water, a stable, and a springhouse.[50] The main house has a defined yard area and is connected to the wharves by a series of paths, ditches, gates, and fences. Shovel tests exposed a mixture of charcoal, tabby, sand and brick rubble, embedded in a hard baked clay substrate, suggesting that the entire eastern edge of the property was used for shipyard industrial activities. Could this be the location of furnaces and burning related to shipyard tasks such as steaming frames and tarring and pitching ships hulls? James Stewart complains in his letters about the shipyard work he detested "since they are planking a 90-gun ship where we kiln the plank in hot wet sand over a large furnace where we go in to shovel on & off the sand which is sometimes so hot that we stay in 5 minutes."[51] This noisy working area of the shipyard with its smell of pitch and the heat from furnaces or kilns (especially during the summer months), and other noxious fumes, would be situated away from the main house.

How does this fit into spatial considerations of a shipyard layout? Historical sources routinely discuss the unhealthfulness of living around a working shipyard. The Hobcaw work area would have been conveniently located along the water's edge on a tidal creek, where workers could douse fires or even dispose of shipbuilding refuse. Shipyard workers could use the deeper, more accessible water wharves at the northern end of the property to launch or haul up ships for repair or to unload cargoes. The shallow area may have been the ideal mudflat for careening vessels for repair work.

Domestic activity of some kind took place closer to the northern end of the property, to the right of the Hernandezes' main house and close to the water. Higher concentrations of cultural materials like ceramics, glassware, and bone are evident, especially along the 586E gridline in the northeastern lot, where the crew elected to excavate units at five-meter intervals. Feature 3 (Unit 487N 581E) revealed an extremely dense cultural deposit and offered the highest quantity of bone except for the shovel tests around Feature 100. A greater volume of brick rubble and oyster shell was also present in much higher weight volumes in test pits on both the 586E and 596E gridlines within this lot. This may have been a refuse area situated close to the shore but far from the main Pritchard house, as shown on the historic plats during their occupation.

On the western perimeter, high volumes of slag and iron fragments suggest the location of auxiliary industries. Workers would have included ropewalkers, block makers, riggers, mastmen, sailmakers, smiths, founders, braziers, coopers, and tanners. Ship chandlers provided nails, bolts, hinges, and anchors, while butchers, bakers, and brewers all contributed to the daily lives of the shipyard laborers. The popular task system (giving slaves free time after they had completed a certain number of assigned plantation tasks) practiced on Charleston plantations may have allowed slaves time to express their cultural identity, unlike the system at a shipyard, which was more akin to industrial labor and followed a stricter time schedule. The extreme paucity in the archaeological record of colonoware, a colonial-era pottery associated with plantation slave manufacturing, also reflects a different aspect of slave shipyard culture. According to probate records for the Hobcaw families, the shipyard always had relatively small slave communities living on the property. These slaves' lifestyles probably were different from those of the vast slave communities on the lowcountry plantations where colonoware is so prevalent in the archaeological record. The implications of the archaeological record are that slaves in the Hobcaw shipyard did not make colonoware, either because they did not have the time to do it or because there were ample European ceramics available from vessels that visited the yard.

Two categories of artifacts possibly associated with shipyard slaves are glass tools and glass beads. It is likely that these were useful for cutting canvass, rigging lines, and scoring timbers much the way a pocket knife or utility knife is used today. Other sources of information about the African connection to these tools include documentation about the use of broken bottles by Africans during the Middle Passage to shave traditional designs in their hair. The practice of using broken glass as a razor was common in the Bahamas until the 1930s. In Louisiana, John Hulbert, a former tenant of Oakley plantation, recalled that glass tools were used to smooth axe and hoe handles. He further commented that only certain people on a plantation had the skill to break glass in a certain way to make a tool. His descriptions suggest that the production of these tools was a skill not shared by the entire tenant population.[52]

The use of a glass tool in a shipyard, while possibly a cultural item associated with African heritage, may reflect Europeans' hesitation to provide slave craftsmen with knives or other potentially dangerous weapons, especially in the tension-filled lowcountry atmosphere after the Stono Rebellion in 1739. A South Carolina archaeologist, Eric Poplin, investigated the ethnographic record to confirm the use of glass as tools at a variety of European and North American nineteenth-century working sites. His informants confirmed repeatedly that the glass shards were ideal as woodworking tools. They added that they generally selected thick shards, such as from a bottle base, with steep edge angles as the ideal shape. Glass tools were usually stored at the site where they were used, beneath an outbuilding or in a nearby tree. They were expedient and cheap tools. Informants even judged these tools to be more efficient than metal items such as drawknives and planes.[53]

The diet of the slaves and shipyard workers is evident from diagnostic faunal material and included deer (*Odocuileus viginianus*), cow (*Bos taurus*), pig (*Sus scrofa*), goat (*Capra hircus hircus*), and bird (*Aves*). Some long bones are cut, suggesting that the material found was dietary refuse. Unworn molars and unfused bones reveal that the animals were young, further supporting the dietary role of these remains. Bird bones, including those of robins and crows and of water birds such as herons or egrets were found among the faunal remains.

The 2004–2005 archaeological investigations provided a greater quantity of diagnostic cultural material, allowing researchers to establish mean dates for the most intensive period of occupation of the project area and tying it solidly into the 1700s. The period 1760–1775 is represented by thirteen ceramic types. Pipe-bore diameters provide an intensive occupation date of 1721.4 through 1764.1. Glassware dates span 1742.2 to 1827.7. The overall estimate of the mean date for the most intensive occupation, based on a combination of these three sets of diagnostic data (ceramics, pipes, and glassware), is 1727.6–1806.6. During this time period, 1727–1806, the property was occupied by the Quelch family (1709–1753; Benjamin, Elizabeth; then Andrew), John Rose and James Stewart (1753–1769; first described as a shipyard at this time); Begbie and Manson (1769–1778); and finally the Pritchards in 1791, who also owned Fairbanks Plantation. Paul Pritchard's son owned Fairbanks Shipyard on the banks of the Wando River during the early 1800s. All these shipwrights owned slaves, who represented an important labor partnership in aiding the shipwrights in their rapid upwardly mobile trajectory in Charleston society. The material culture on the site thus represents a vignette of English (John Rose), Scottish (James Stewart), and Irish (Paul Pritchard) immigrant history in Charleston.

Archaeological investigations at Hobcaw shipyard correlate with the historical record, showing increased occupation and wealth in the mid-1700s, at the time of the Stewart-Rose partnership. The artifacts, especially ceramics and pipes, in archaeological deposits show the period from the mid- to the late 1700s as one of the most intensive occupation of the shipyard. Other characteristic of the shipyard ceramic assemblage mirror those of other 1700s sites in the Charleston area. Chinese porcelain became more readily available by the second half of the eighteenth century and was affordable to the middle and lower classes, particularly in a major port like Charleston. Archaeologists, like Martha Zierden and Ron Anthony of the Charleston Museum, have noted a great variety of types and styles of historic ceramics in lowcountry assemblages on other sites in the downtown area and on plantations along the river systems.[54]

4.

From African Canoe to Carolina Crew

Throughout the eighteenth century local newspaper advertisements explicitly announced where slaves came; typical notices referred to "a fine cargo of healthy young slaves, just imported from the Gold Coast and Angola"; "mostly of the MASSE CONGO country"; or "from WHYDAH on the Gold Coast."[1] Many of the cultures from which slaves were imported had extensive craft and trade skills well known to the Europeans who explored or colonized Africa. Planters made efforts to import slaves from areas of West Africa where rice, cotton, and indigo were grown.[2] Water skills like swimming, free diving, sailing, paddling, and rowing can also be added to this laundry list of less visible cultural contributions to the colonial world. The planters perpetuated the African boating and labor tradition in ports and along river systems of colonial Africa.

Canoe men, primarily fishermen, were indispensable to the Portuguese ships sailing the rough surf along the coastline of West Africa as early as the 1500s. By 1650 the canoe men serving the Dutch, French, and English trade ships totaled 350, and by 1790 they totaled 1,000. These canoeists were a workforce that was an integral part of the operating procedures of the transatlantic trade. They received wages as employees, ferried passengers and cargoes to and from the beaches, and were frequently implicated in illegal trade activities. Companies kept careful records of disbursements headed "canoe men hire," enumerating the wages paid to "slave canoe men" and "free canoe men." The canoe men were recorded as going on strike for better payment and through time rose in rank and status by engaging in slave trading themselves. During the prolonged Anglo-Dutch Wars of the seventeenth and eighteenth centuries, canoe men became seriously embroiled in international conflicts.[3]

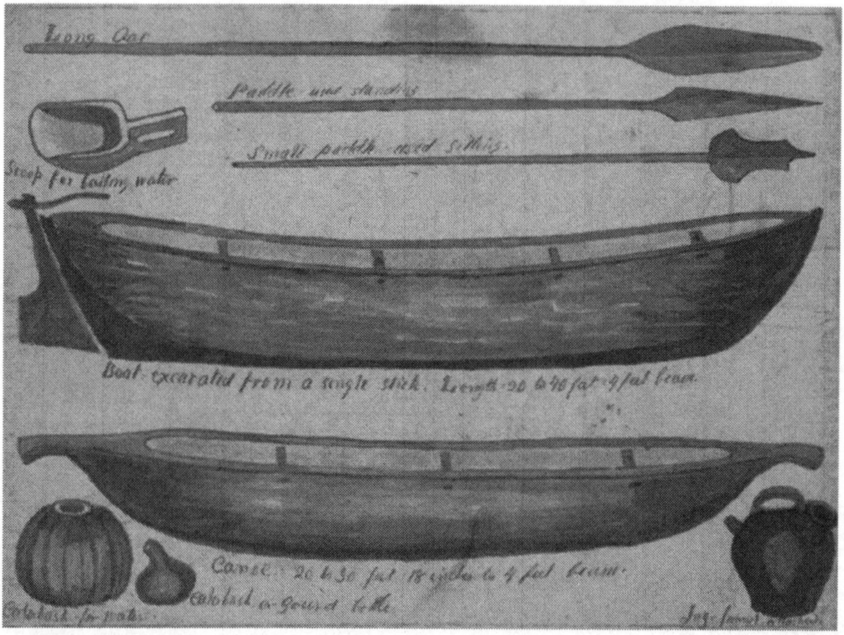

Figure 5. Two African dugout canoes with accessories. Courtesy of Special Collections, University of Virginia.

The slaves that the West Indian settlers brought with them originated from a variety of coastal, lake, and rive-system regions of Africa where boats were everyday commodities used in a manner similar to the way they were used by Native Americans. Rivers connected inland communities with ports and "sea-people" navigated up and down the African shore from the Gold Coast to Angola in brilliantly colored boats decorated with crescent moons, stars, and sea-life symbols drawn from their mythology.[4] The canoe form was one of the most popular and functional craft types in Africa.

European visitors to West Africa left accounts that describe log canoes that varied in size from small fishing canoes carrying a crew of one to canoes of more than eighty feet in length. The small canoes were paddled by children and adults. In one report a traveler remarks on "a canoe, paddled by four young boys, not much older than seven years of age, and steered with a paddle by a man in the stern."[5] They also reported seeing smaller canoes paddled by solitary females or males, marveling at the dexterity of these canoeists. In one report they describe a typical solitary fishing scene:

> The appearance of the canoes, as well as the agility of their tenants is remarkable. The former are not more than six to eight feet in length, fourteen to

> sixteen inches in width, and from four to six inches in depth. When the fishing man sits in the canoe, as we sit on horseback, his leg at either side being the guiding power. The line with its beardless hook, having a shrimp for bait, is played up and down with one hand, whilst the other he now and then seizes a large ladle and bails out the boat with a rapidity of motion that at first site seems really ludicrous.[6]

There are descriptions of various practices of paddling. Canoe men propelled small, single-person canoes with their hands while "they will use one foot to bale water out of the canoe"; sometimes the canoes were "propelled with the feet almost as fast as the paddle." To get into a smaller canoe quickly, if there was more than one person on board, a native would swim toward the canoe and roll himself over the gunwale in a horizontal position, the other people in the boat leaning over to the opposite side to prevent it tipping.[7]

Fishing trips often ended in canoe surfing races "on top of the surging billows which broke on the sea shore," with the natives described as having qualities of "nimbleness and security of ducks." The surfing races took place along selected stretches of coastline chosen for their continuous long swells, which lasted for several hundred yards. It was amazing to the European viewers that "no one ever drowned . . . [because] like the majority of coast negroes they may be reckoned amphibious."[8]

In much the same way that fanatical surfers today are not deterred by sharks, neither, it appears, were these fishermen surfers. On some occasions, a traveler remarked "when the fisherman is hauling on the line [the shark] comes in sight of the larger bait of the negro leg, and chops it off without remorse. Even though the victim died—it did not diminish the number of canoes riding the waves."[9]

"These canoe labors constitute the whole of the work done by males," commented a European. The larger canoes were "scooped out of the single trunk of a tree. Some of these canoes are from thirty five to thirty six feet in length and of five foot in beam, and four in depth. They are propelled by oars as well as sails and are schooner-rigged."[10] Some were designed with elaborate features resembling a quarterdeck and fo'castle. Canoes on the Bonny and Calabar Rivers in the Eastern delta of the Niger had cooking hearths and arrangements for stowage and sleeping mats for the crew.[11] The larger canoes were built for the calm waters of the estuaries and rivers and were often intricately carved and painted; others were used for warfare and carried as many as 120 warriors armed with spears (*assegaais*), shields, and arrows. Among the African people who owned these fleets, warfare took a distinctive form that can be differentiated from land warfare. These canoes were not simply used to transport land

Figure 6. Navigating the surf in an African canoe. Courtesy of Special Collections, University of Virginia.

troops but merit a designation as naval. Evidence of canoe warfare is described in the early accounts by the Portuguese in the Sierra Leone River.[12]

In shallow rivers and lagoons, canoes were often punted and poled instead of rowed. Boat makers designed sails made from grass fiber or palm fronds woven together. African precolonial boatbuilders were specialists in their trade, living in the forests that provided their raw materials. Here clients visited them; sometimes they worked from "children's boats" sent to them as models. The life expectancy of a lagoon or lake canoe was two to three years, but the more costly and carefully made canoes for sea fishing or coastal voyaging, when properly treated and patched, were used up for to fifteen years.[13]

In the seventeenth and eighteenth centuries organized European expeditions into northwest Africa concentrated on the Gambia and Senegal Rivers. Travelers provided numerous short accounts or compiled their accounts along with those of others.[14] Gold Coast traders who visited the Dutch ships at the beginning of the seventeenth century observed that "the people that dwell within the land can hardly brooke the seas . . . but their rowers and pilots that bring them aboard are hardie enough and never sicke, by reason of their daily using the sea."[15] The people of Senegal during that time period "fished three, four, and five leagues to sea" and were "expert and able swimmers." One source suggests that the intrepid African sailors of the Gold Coast ventured not only into the Bight of Guinea but even to Angola. A special kind of biscuit was baked that remained in good condition for three or four months "to victual the canoes in which they make coasting voyages as far as Angola."[16]

There are descriptions of how Africans used canoes to transport slaves from inland areas down the rivers to the port cities. Two Frenchmen, the Chevalier des Marchais and the Sieur d'Elbée, described the boats they saw and how they were used along the coastline and on the rivers of Angola and the Congo. Africans had both smaller canoes and large boats. The travelers described the latter as "made up of the trunk of the *Likondo,* or *Alikunda,* a Tree of a monstrous size; for that one of them will carry about two hundred Persons. In rowing they do not rest their Oars on the Boat's Side, but hold them at Liberty in their hands: They also steer with them. When they fight on the Water, they lay down their Oar, and take their Bow."[17] On another occasion the travelers encountered "two Bark-log" canoes on the beach. They explained that these "Pieces of Wood, tied close together in the Nature of a Raft or Float, the two ends pointed, and raised on each side with Pieces for Gunnels about seven Inches high." Mungo Park referred to boats in Africa made from two trees that were "rendered concave and joined together . . . the junction being exactly across the middle of the canoe" and being "long and disproportionately narrow." There are descriptions of a "flying ferry" drawn from one side of the river to the other by means of a rope. One such ferry allowed several persons and horses to cross the Niger River.[18]

Travelers noted that communities in Gold Coast African towns such as Axim, Boutroe, Tacorary, Commendo, Cormentin, and Wineba were well known for their canoe-making and handling skills. The travelers were intrigued by the manufacturing process and described it in great detail:

> When the Trunk of the Tree is cut to the Length they design, they hollow it as much as they can with these crooked knives, and they burn it out by Degrees, until it is reduced to the intended Cavity and Thickness, which they then Scrape and Plane with other small tools of their Invention, both within and without, leaving it sufficient Thickness, so as not to Split when loaded. The Bottom is made almost flat, and the sides somewhat rounded, so that it is always narrower, just at the Top, and bellies out a little lower, that it may carry more Sail. The Head and Stern are raised long, and somewhat hooked, very sharp at the End, that several men may lift them on Occasion, to lay it up ashore and turn it upside down, so that they make it as light as possible.[19]

African boatbuilders sold these craft to the Europeans and to their neighbors. The largest could carry up to twelve tons of goods. The Mina men were repeatedly assessed as the most skilful boatmen; they could manage the canoes with heavy loads "over the most dangerous bars and raging waters." They would beach the canoes with great dexterity in the most dangerous sea and wind conditions, and were "used to such incidents, and were excellent swimmers and divers."[20] In South Guinea, the traveler Jean Barbot admitted:

> It was very diverting to me to see great numbers of both sexes, indifferently mixed together, playing with much activity and dexterity among the surges of the sea, about the shore, some on pieces of timber, others on bundles of rushes, made fast under their stomachs, the better to learn to swim, others ducking under the water, and continuing there for a considerable time, the Blacks on the coast looking on it as perfection in a Boy or Girl to swim well, which may be of use to them sometime in their life.[21]

The paddlers in the larger canoes were seated in a variety of configurations of two, three, five, eleven, or fifteen. They sat in the canoes in pairs on benches nailed at equal distances athwart, except for the man steering at the stern. European were intrigued by the Africans' use of paddles instead of oars, "made like a Spade, having a handle about the Same Length with which, paddling the Water with an under stroke, they paddle the Canoa in a very swift course."[22]

Travelers expressed surprise at the great maneuverability and speed of even the largest canoes. Even though the canoes were light, the freeboard was so low that the boatmen sat half underwater. The paddlers sat in the middle of the boat on a small stool with a steerman at the stern. These canoas, they claimed, "flew like Arrows along the Water, so that no Bark nor Shallop can come-up with them, especially if the Sea be smooth and calm."[23] If the seas were rough the canoes would often roll over, but the Africans were extremely dexterous in righting the boat, bailing out the water and continuing their voyage.

During long voyages to Angola, in southern Africa, they utilized masts and sails, oars and paddles. The sails were made of rush-mats, "a Sort of Cloth of the Bark of Trees, having long hairy Threads, like the Cocoa-Tree, which they spin and weave into Canvas, and their Rigging is of Palm-tree Yarn." Boats were painted inside and out and adorned with "fetishes and idols" such as dried corn and several dry heads of lions, goats, monkeys, and other animals. If the voyage was long, they often hung a dead animal, such as a goat, off the stern. Pleasure canoes were made for important European officials. One such example had curtains and a large blue and gold awning decorated with silver and gold fringe. Turkish carpets covered the "handsome seats."[24] Holman described a boat that used seventeen paddles and had chairs fixed to a platform in the forward part.

These ornate canoes were sufficiently intriguing that travelers sent home model canoes along with numerous African-made items such as spears, fishing lines, stone slings made from the fiber of a bark tree, armlets, bracelets, knives made out of an old iron hoop, and monkey skins.[25]

In Calabar, the traveler Jean Barbot reported on the canoes used in warfare or in areas where they might encounter hostile communities. These canoes were much larger than the others, being seventy or eighty feet in length (enough to accommodate seventy or eighty men) and eight feet wide. The canoe men hung shields at the bow and javelins along the sides of the boat. Features on the boats included a hearth, a quarterdeck made of reeds, a shelter for "principal persons," and a variety of provisions that usually included yams, bananas, chickens, hogs, goats, sheep, palm wine, and palm oil.[26]

Boat trips on rivers often included both whites and blacks. The numbers and the ethnic identities of river travelers were listed in reports. Captain Stibbs supervised a river expedition in December 1723 that was sent to collect gold at James Fort. The expedition included five large canoes named the *Chandos,* the *Royal Africa,* the *Expedition,* the *Gambia,* and the *Discovery.* These canoes ranged between thirty-three and forty-two feet long and between three and six feet in width. Each carried between nine and twelve people. The composition of the expedition was fifteen whites, thirty African men (Cape Coasters and Grometta s), four women slaves as cooks, three boys, and one linguist, who was described as a Portuguese black. The expedition was an arduous adventure. The five canoes were frequently loaded and unloaded to be hauled over sandbars. At dangerous waterfalls or rapids the crew carried the canoes over land, on quite a few occasions being chased by herds of wild elephants. Occasionally they would camp on a sandbar waiting for rains to make the river deeper, sending crew member into surrounding villages to buy food items like chickens and eggs.[27]

In addition to the Africans' boating and surfing skills, their swimming abilities also fascinated European explorers, traders, and colonizers. The Flemish explorer Pieter de Marees expounded on the swimming abilities of the Gold Coast people and observed that they could "swim very fast, generally easily outdoing people of our nation in swimming and diving." It was evident from these reports that Africans executed a form of freestyle stroke, whereas European did a breaststroke or dog paddle. Jean Barbot commented, "blacks of Mina, outdo all others at the coast in dexterity of swimming, throwing one [arm] after another forward, as if they were paddling, and not extending their arm equally, and striking with both together, as Europeans do."[28]

They swam underwater equally efficiently, amazing the Scottish explorer Mungo Park with their lung capacity. He described how one fisherman dove underwater in the Senegal River to set his fish traps "for such a length of time that I thought he had drowned himself." He also described how, on another occasion, a canoe carrying soldiers overturned and the natives dived down, recovering muskets and a man's body. The rest of the party from the capsized boat drowned because they could not swim. Swimming and diving underwater was a way to deceive and steal from Europeans. At the Grain Coast (now Liberia), a traveler, Johann van Lubelfing, witnessed an occasion where some natives jumped into the water with stolen beer tankards in the hands and helmets on their heads, swimming underwater to a getaway boat provided by an accomplice.[29]

Diving was also a useful labor skill. Another traveler, D. O. Dapper, described Africans diving for gold nuggets that accumulated on riverbeds at the foot of waterfalls. One of the French Huguenot artists who accompanied Sir Francis Drake to the West Indies in the late sixteenth century illustrated how enslaved African divers on Margarita Island off the coast of Venezuela harvested pearl oysters. When diving, they carried "hoop-net" baskets fastened to the canoes by ropes. He described how divers collected pearl oysters from the ocean bed, placed the oysters in the baskets, and pulled the basket to the surface with great effort.[30]

Along the Ivory Coast, native swimmers provided entertainment for European spectators. William Bosman explained, "You are probably aquainted with the expert Swimming and Diving of these Negroes which I have several times seen with Suprize. Whenever they were on Board, and I threw a string of Coral, or anything else into the Sea, one would immediately dive after it, and tho' almost to the bottom fetch it up again. They seldom missed of, and were sure of what they brought up as Reward."[31]

Swimming and boating in rivers of Africa was associated with the constant danger posed by crocodiles and hippos. One European explorer exclaimed that on the Niger River, "An incredible number of hippopotami arose very near us, and came plashing, snorting and plunging, all around the canoe, and placed us in imminent danger." He elaborated, "Our people who have never in all their lives been exposed in a canoe to such huge and formidable beasts, trembled in fear and apprehension, and absolutely wept aloud."[32] Captain Jobson related stories of his trip along the Gambra River, describing how the natives told many "lamentable stories of their friends being devoured" by the *Bumbo* [crocodiles]. These crocodiles had a strong musk scent and "lay in great Companies upon the Sands, and would avoid the Sight and Noise of Men as much as Snakes do in England, but were bolder in deep Water." One of the methods by which the Africans crossed rivers in a small canoe was to lead an ox as crocodile bait into the water by the horns, with one member holding the ox close to the boat, another pulling the tail of the ox, and a third standing up with bow ready and charged to shoot any approaching crocodile. Frequently, other crew had to jump into the water to pull and push the boat along. When Europeans accompanied natives on these trip, they were encouraged to push the boat along with the knowledge that "Whites shine more in the water than the Blacks do, therefore *Bumbos* [crocodiles] would seize them first."[33]

African Canoes: The Archaeological and Ethnographic Record

Africa's oldest known boat, named the "Dufuna Canoe," was discovered near the region of the River Yobe. Fulani herdsmen discovered the canoe in May 1987, in Dufuna Village, while digging a well. The canoe's "almost black wood" was identified as African mahogany. Various radiocarbon tests indicate that the canoe is more than eight thousand years old, making it the oldest known canoe in the archaeological record of Africa. Little is known of the period to which the boat belongs. In archaeological terms it is described as an early phase of the Later Stone Age, which began more than 12,000 years ago and ended with the appearance of pottery. The lab results redefined the prehistory of African water transport, ranking the Dufuna canoe as the world's third-oldest known dugout. Older dugouts had been found in Pesse, the Netherlands, and in Noyen-sur-Seine, France. Specialists believe that "evidence of an eight-thousand-year-old tradition of boatbuilding in Africa throws cold water on the assumption that maritime transport developed much later there in comparison with Europe." Peter Breunig of the University of Frankfurt, in Germany, an archaeologist involved in the project, says the canoe's age "forces a reconsideration of Africa's role in the history of water transport." It shows, he added, "that the cultural history of Africa was not determined by Near Eastern and European influences but took its own, in many cases parallel, course." Breunig, added that the canoe even outranked in style European finds of similar age. "The bow and stern are both carefully worked to points, giving the boat a notably more elegant form," compared to "the dugout made of conifer wood from Pesse in the Netherlands, whose blunt ends and thick sides seem crude." To judge by its stylistic sophistication, he reasons, "It is highly probable that the Dufuna boat does not represent the beginning of a tradition, but had already undergone a long development, and that the origins of water transport in Africa lie even further back in time."[34]

Ethnographers like Allison Gray, working for the Arts and Culture Program in Ghana, and Jojada Verrips, from the Anthropology Department at the University of Amsterdam, studied contemporary watercraft of northwest Africa, many built in much the same way as their prototypes from the 1600s.[35] Their research focused how the canoe, as an art form, intertwined social, economic, and religious beliefs. Verrips argues that canoes are the succinct symbolic expressions of a wide range of relations, identifications, and sympathies of their owners/users with things, fellow human beings, and ideas. The decorations are chosen from "a big reservoir of possibilities and carefully composed into what one could call a distinctive, decorative Gestalt, so that each canoe gets, just like its owner/user, a recognizable identity or 'individuality' amongst other, similarly treated canoes." He suggests that a beach with moored canoes can be considered as a revealing manifestation of the social community of the fishermen. The canoes have many different roles: they are messengers and talk on behalf of their owners; they show their owners' "mindscape"; and they convey subtle information how different users relate to one another and perceive their world.

Gray provides a detailed account of the manufacturing process and describes the high status of the canoe builders and repairmen within their communities. These men are creators who are considered almost religious leaders. She describes the tools they use, the building sequence, and the language they use to describe parts of the canoe and their decorative techniques. She observed and questioned fishermen about their ideas regarding the role of boats in the community. Ethnographic studies of these contemporary African boats may help researchers develop hypotheses about how enslaved colonial people manufactured, valued, and personified their canoes.

5.

The Plantation Patroon

During a boat trip down the Ashley River, Juba, the head oarsman, led his fellow slaves in a song about the boat *Neely,* which was named for the young mistress, Cornelia, who was aboard. Later the song shifted focus to Cornelia's suitor, who was also aboard, acknowledging his presence and complimenting him as a possible captain for the plantation rowboat:

> Hi de good boat Neely?
> She row bery fast, Miss Neely!
> Aint no boat like Miss Neely,
> Ho yoi'!
> Who gawing to row wid Miss Neely?
> Can't catch dis boat Neely—
> Nobody show de face wid Neely
> Ho yoi'!
> Maybe Maus Lewis take de oar for Neely,
> Bery handsome boat Miss Neely!
> Maus Lewis nice Captain for Neely,
> Hoi Yoi![1]

River and waterborne activities were an integral part of the lowcountry plantation's daily routine just as they were in the West Indies plantations. An early historian for the Royal Government wrote: "The oldest plantations were upon rivers, a waterfront indeed, and a landing were essential to such establishments, for it must have the periago for plantation purposes and the trim sloop and large cypress canoes for the masters use."[2]

Figure 7. Sailing pirogue in West Africa. Courtesy of Special Collections, University of Virginia.

Slave boatmen formed the crews for a variety of different vessel types, including canoes, flats, and sailing vessels. Planters gave their boatmen uniforms and the title "patroon" and advertised them in newspapers as valuable commodities. The tone of newspaper advertisements suggests that masters recognized that some expertise was involved in the occupation of "boatman," skills that slaves either brought with them from their former lives in Africa or acquired while working on plantations in the colonies. Planters frequently made a distinction between their slave's skills at inland boating and seamanship. Sometime they noted the types of vessels with which a particular slave had a familiarity. For examples, advertisements listed "a fine strong Negro Man that has been used to the sea, or to go in Pettigua" and a "Lad chiefly used to row in Boats";[3] they also emphasized different levels of skill: "middling good boatman,"[4] "pretty good sailor,"[5] "remarkable good fisherman,"[6] "a good sailor."[7]

European visitors to plantations were intrigued by the canoes as well as by the slave crews. William Howard Russell, a correspondent for the London *Times*, described this Elliot family plantation scenario:

> Spite of wind and tideway, it came rapidly, and soon approaches us, pulled by 6 powerful Negroes, attired in red flannel jackets and white straw hats with broad ribands. The craft itself-a kind of monster canoe, some 45 feet long, narrow, wall-sided, with high bow and raised stern-lay deep in the water, for there were extra Negroes for fishing, servants, baskets of provisions,

Figure 8. Plantation sailing boat. Used by permission of the Charleston Museum.

water buckets, stone jars of less innocent drinking, and abaft there was a knot of great strong planters—Elliots all—cousins, uncles, and brothers.[8]

One boat used in these races was thirty-seven feet in length and was described as having a straight keel and sheer line that promised great speed. It was deemed unsuitable for anything but racing and was prone to capsizing in anything but capable hands. These slave crews raced plantation boats and met regularly for local races and speed trials. As John Grayson elaborated: "Then, mile after mile, the toiling crews stript of jacket and vest urged each other to desparate exertions, while the sweat rolled down their faces and the speed of the boats was quadruple. At the end of the race the victorious oarsmen boasted of their exploits and taunted their defeated antagonists."[9]

As the Sea Islands were settled, planters began to rely on their supply of country-born Africans who had adapted to the colonial setting and who oversaw labor operations on plantations. Compared to other work on a plantation, the position of skilled boatman was a superior one among the slave community and in the eyes of the planter. A patroon was also responsible for the other boat hands and trained them in rowing techniques and rowing songs. There seems to have been a certain pride attached to this position. Oarsmen who did not exert themselves sufficiently were berated through song. On a boat trip on Edisto

Island, the leading oarsman, named Big Mouth Joe, scolded his lazy crew members, singing:

> One time upon dis ribber
> Long time ago—
> Mass Ralph e' had a nigger,
> Long time ago—
> Da nigger had no merit,
> Long time ago—
> De nigger could'nt row wid spirit,
> Long time ago,
> and now dere is in dis boat, ah
> a nigger dat I see—
> Wha' is good for nothing shoat, ah,
> ha, ha, ha, he—
> Da nigger's weak like water—
> Ha, ha, ha, he—
> 'E can't crow half quarter,
> Ha, ha, ha, he—
> Cuss de nigger-cuss'e libber,
> Ha, ha, ha, he.[10]

Work songs in the field or on boats were often composed spontaneously by slaves as outlets for emotional release through innuendo, metaphor, and circumlocution and promoted communal solidarity.

Slaves not only crewed on the boats but also built and cared for them. Planters gave their South Carolina slaves an extraordinary measure of independence. This was particularly true of the boatmen. Nothing inverted the "normal" master-to-slave relationship so profoundly and regularly as the operation of the plantation schooner. The technical skill and value of the patroons gave them a great deal of authority. Many a planter "waited for wind and tide—and the boatman." The need to establish a balance between the decision to grant these freedoms and the need to use the slaves' waterborne skills to conduct everyday tasks resulted in tensions on a number of plantations.[11]

In his account books, Henry Laurens placed the value of "the schooner *Baker* & 4 Negroes on board her" at £2,600. By way of comparison, he places the value of the Wambaw Plantation of 791,500 acres, with dams, buildings, cattle, hogs, horses, at £10,000. The plantation schooner *Wambaw,* a fifteen-ton (15,240.7 kg) and plantation boat *Baker* were valued at £1,200. Plantation correspondence reveals the reality of a situation described as a crisis, where there was "upwards of four blacks to one white person."[12] The letter books of Henry

Figure 9. Plantation rowboat. Used by permission of the Charleston Museum.

Figure 10. Man in canoe transporting barrels. Used by permission of the Charleston Museum.

Figure 11. Fishing vessel, ca. late 1800s or early 1900s. Used by permission of the Charleston Museum.

Laurens provide particularly interesting insights into the role of these boatmen and the associated plantation politics. In one letter to John Loveday, Laurens gives instructions about making slave clothing, noting that his four boatmen should wear Jack Robbins blue pea jackets, trousers of brown cloth, and a "blanket Surtout" in contrast to the usual brown clothing.[13] This difference in clothing probably enabled the overseer to make a quick distinction between boatmen and other slaves. It also served symbolically to separate the two groups socially, creating a kind of plantation slave class structure. "Don't let the boat Negroes go amongst the Plantation Negroes" was one of the instructions most frequently delivered by Laurens to his overseers at Mepkin Plantation on the Cooper River.[14] The boatmen, with their relative freedom, were important sources of information about the outside world because of their access to port markets. Planters viewed them as a worldly and potentially disruptive influence on the other slaves.

In another letter Laurens wrote to John Smith at Mepkin: "Load the boat as well as you can & take care to prevent any intercourse between Boat and Plantation Negroes and let me know how Abram the Patroon of the Boat behaves."[15] As boat traffic proliferated on the rivers in the lowcountry, there were increasing concerns about pilfering from boats by slave crews and also the sale of goods by slaves to other slaves in Charleston markets. Slave marketing initiatives were facilitated through the boatmen, despite the restrictions of slavery. This practice limited business opportunities for urban white merchants and cast suspicions on the planters and their boatmen.

Plantation documents for Mepkin Plantation on the Cooper River make references to several slave boatmen who interacted directly with Henry Laurens.[16] It was a master-and-slave relationship that generated tremendous tensions for the planter. Despite Laurens's caution, his slaves still had great latitude in their comings and goings. Laurens describes how Abram the boatman was very "sly and artful" and notes that it required all his "skill to . . . counteract him." Abram had some very "pernicious connections" with slaves in Charleston that were of concern to Laurens. On one occasion Abram failed to board the plantation schooner before it left Georgetown, and Laurens began to lose his patience. Although he initiated the process for selling the troublesome slave, Laurens seemed to change his mind and instead promoted him from boatman to patroon. Laurens still suspected Abram, even in this new position, of selling plantation wood and trading with other slaves. The ambivalent relationship between master and slave boatman is reflected in what Laurens wrote about Abram's assets and problem areas when he intended to sell him. Abram's good qualities were his "woodworking, boating, whitewashing, plastering, and horsemanship skills tempered by a dose of healthy, strong constitution, and a willingness to work hard to avoid being chastised." His bad qualities were constant deception, feigned illness, pilfering, ingratitude, womanizing, and disobedience.[17]

Even the slave patroon Scaramouch, who was in charge of Henry Laurens's boats, was a problem. Laurens portrayed him as a skillful boatman but also a rebellious troublemaker and an obvious risk. Like Abram, Scaramouch was promoted and placed in charge of one of Laurens's coastal vessels. Tom Peas, another valuable slave boat captain, died a year later, much to the distress of the Mepkin overseer, who wrote that he was "at loss for a patroon and white men are not to be hired." Through this correspondence, Henry Laurens provides some insights into the trusts, fears, and sentiments that characterized his relationships with his boatmen. They evidently felt they had sufficient status within the plantation system to make demands and promises and to argue vehemently for their needs and wants. Laurens considered good boatmen so valuable to that he was prepared to bargain and compromise to keep them happy, giving the slaves considerable leverage in their bondage situation. He evidently built canoes at Mepkin Plantation for slave use and instructed his overseer, John Smith, at one time to make "three more besides one of your own."[18]

Fear of the independence of plantation patroons on the rivers around Charleston were considerable, and there was a movement toward having boats captained by Europeans. In 1744, white patroons claimed that all slave crews threatened their jobs and petitioned the legislature to relieve the situation.[19] Planters, in contrast, claimed they could not find experienced Europeans to undertake this role occupied by slaves when needed. As Henry Laurens reported: "Achilles [his slave patroon at the time] is capable enough to bring the Schooner to town but it would be highly improper as well as illegal to put such confidence in a Negro, therefore I request further aid to procure a white man to bring her round who may if he is properly recommended."[20]

The petition by the white boatmen had no apparent impact, because slaves continued to dominate the Charleston waters. An investigation by the South Carolina Council into allegations of a slave conspiracy on the Eastern Branch of the Cooper River in 1750 revealed that of the eight plantation boats that plied between Charleston and the inland settlements, five had all-slave crews with a slave patroon. Only three had a white patroon at the helm.[21] Plantation owners occasionally resorted to small-scale bribery of the officials to help them obtain permits or registrations for boats captained by slaves. On occasion, boat registration officials negotiated with planters about facilitating illegal slave captains while registering under the name of a white captain.[22]

Plantation boats proliferated on the inland waterways. South Carolina was an active part of the colonial carrying trade, and Charleston merchants were constantly exploring options and bargains in the home shipping market.[23] Governor James Glen, writing to the Lords Commissioners for Trade and Plantations in England, noted that the "Cooper River appears sometimes a kind of floating market, and we have numbers of canoes, boats, and pettyaguas that ply incessantly, bringing down the country produce to town, and returning with such necessarys as are wanted by the planters."[24] Several colonial planters were also prominent merchants and active business partners in the seagoing trade. In this capacity they extended their labor resources by hiring out their boat slaves as crew to coastal vessels. Henry Laurens sent two African seamen to work aboard the schooner *Brothers Endeavor*, bound for Sunbury and Alatamaha in Georgia to pick up cargoes of rice and shingles and then for Jamaica. The cargo was to be bartered for cash or "neat full proof Rum, the very Finest and Dryest Muscovado Sugar, Melossas, . . . and the best Coffee." Laurens instructed the captain that the two African seamen were entitled to no wages, only clothing and provisions, because they were his slaves. This appears to have been a fairly regular practice among planters. Laurens advised Magnus Watson, the master of his schooner, to "Compel the slaves to be good Ship keepers and not to suffer them to wander from the vessel in this [Charleston] or any other port." The colony's growing shipping required offshore crews, and the use of slaves was a profitable venture.[25]

Some slaves had enough leeway in bondage to seek out employment opportunities, including employment as boat crews for other boats and ships, beyond crewing within their own plantation milieu. This allowed them to provide services as interpreters, guides, or traders to ships' captains using their own boats. Slaves were allowed to "go wither and work where they pleased" with little control by owners, who did not mind as long as the slave gave him a share of the profits. An act "for the better ordering and governing of Negroes and other slaves [Native Americans] in the province," a *South Carolina Gazette* columnist wrote, would require that all slave sent out have a "certificate, note, or memorandum thereof." It was also lawful for "any person to seize all boats and canoes *belonging* to slaves."[26]

Newspapers described numerous instances of boats used by runaways; in one instance, "two Negroe Women, one with a sucking child, ran away. They took a cypress canoe about twenty five foot long and three foot wide."[27] Another notice describes a runaway as "a short squat Negro named Stephen, [who] was a patroon of a large wood boat."[28] In 1740 an African and a Native American escaped together with the sloop *Mayflower*. They used a cypress boat that was eighteen feet in length. On another occasion five Native Americans "who belonged aboard the Prince of Orange" escaped.[29] Planters warned masters of vessels, whom they cautioned for "harboring, entertaining or carrying off of the said runaway slaves—Bastion of Indian breed and his black wife Lucy";[30] "a young Spanish Indian [who escaped] from the Brigantine *Polly and Fanny*";[31] and "a pettyaugua, carrying about 40 or 50 barrels of rice, and a Negro Man who is a profound sailmaker."[32]

Most slaves who ran away were engaged in maritime occupations or labor projects on the rivers at the time of their escape (or for any number of months or years prior to their escape). Usually they used a river- or oceangoing vessel either as a means of escape or as a way to reach a place of escape. Many advertisements described not only the use of the boat but the assistance given by or an association with slave boatmen or sailors. A review of advertisements for runaway slaves from South Carolina for the period 1732–1784 shows that out of a total of 325 male runaway slaves, 192 were described as having occupational experience connected to boats. The 192 male runaways listed as having one or more skilled occupations in South Carolina had maritime experience. Nearly 60 percent of skilled slaves who were runaways had maritime experience. In fact, slave boatmen accounted for 10 percent of the 1,856 male slaves, skilled or unskilled, who were advertised as runaways in South Carolina.[33]

Over time the seamanship abilities of both Africans and Native Americans and their intimate knowledge of the coastline became a great liability as well as an asset to white Charlestonians. On occasion, ships from the West Indies encountered runaways on the high seas, some in canoes, and attempted to smuggle them into Charleston with the intent of selling them and making a profit.[34] For international rivals like the Spanish, a knowledgeable coastal pilot was a valuable source of strategic information. A slave named Arrah was captured by a French privateer sloop from the schooner belonging to Hugh Cartwright and was encouraged to defect to enemy ranks. He declined and returned to Charleston several years later after his release. For his loyalty to the colony, the Assembly of South Carolina gave him his freedom through a special act. Any other slaves taken by the enemy who escaped and returned to South Carolina thereafter were also awarded their freedom.[35]

In addition to boating and piloting, there were other highly competitive skills as watermen that planters viewed both as recreational and as desirable for their European-educated sons to learn from their slaves. Colonial entertainments included slave swimming, alligator fighting, and rowing and sailing contests. From the time Europeans first arrived in the southern colony, they repeatedly talked about their fears of the larger aquatic fauna. An English sea captain who wrote a poem about everyday life in Charleston included in his litany of horrors a reference to "Frightful creatures in the water, Porpoises, sharks and alligators." These were situations that many Europeans were not familiar with in their past world. Even in the West Indies travelers commented on the dangers, especially that posed by alligators and crocodiles:

> Here are also a great many Alligators and Crocodiles that haunt about this island, and are said to be the most daring in all of West Indies. I have heard of many tricks: as that they have followed a Canoa, and put their Noses in over the Gunnal, with their Jaws wide open, as if ready to devour the Men in it: and that when they have been ashore at night on the Sea, the crocodiles have come in among them, and made them run from their fire, and taken away their meat from them. Therefore when privateers are hunting on the

> island, they always keep centinals out to watch these ravenous creatures, as duly as they do in other places for fear of Enemies, especially in the night, for fear of being devoured in their sleep.[36]

These fears and the worry about one's ability to deal with the alligators were a continual source of paranoia in the colonial and antebellum worlds. Watching slaves compete in physical activities, including wrestling these "frightful creatures," was popular among the Southern planters. Usual activities included traditional blood sports like boxing but also a variety of water sports. Champions from one plantation competed against representatives of other plantations, each representing the honor and prestige of his "master" and quite possibly promoting a sense of plantation community, camaraderie, and allegiance. A variety of traveler and plantation reports suggest that slaves welcomed the opportunity to be involved in spontaneous competition in their leisure time, including horse and boat races. Younger male slaves, especially, delighted in "seeing who could run the fastest, swim the longest, jump the highest, and lift the heaviest objects. The ability to perform well in these physical events also singled them out and gained them the respect of their fellow slaves. One of the ways to attain a degree of status and recognized leadership in the slave quarter community was to be successful on the playing field."[37]

Planters proudly showcased the aquatic skills of their slaves to neighboring planters. These men put the safety of their wives and children, seated in small boats in lowcountry rivers teeming with alligators, in the hands of the plantation patroon. They relied on the patroons to transport their valuable plantation merchandise efficiently and speedily to markets. At a time when most Europeans could not swim except for the dog paddle to save themselves in an emergency, slaves were plantation lifeguards extraordinaire. These water skills made a slave more valuable should the planter wish to sell him or want to promote the competence of his labor force to a prospective merchant considering buying his rice.

The swimming prowess of certain slaves, for example, was discussed by the planter John Clinkscales, who boasted about his slave Essex (Essick). Essex was five feet ten, weighed 190 pounds, and "was as sinewy and active as a Texas pony" on his father's South Carolina plantation, and Clinkscales promoted him as the best swimmer not only on the plantation but in the whole country.[38] Clinkscales stated emphatically that people that had no idea of the pride a slave owner took in the physical strength of his manservants and how much a slave could contribute to the outdoor skill set of a child. Essex, he elaborated, was "a nobleman of the world." He "taught wayward white children to love the truth; he taught me the names and habits of the birds; he taught me to swim, shoot, and ride. He taught me nothing of books, but much of life."[39]

Others extended swimming contests to include fighting sharks, alligators, and manta rays. South Carolina travelogues specifically mention Africans' abilities with sharks and sharks' value as food and medicine and for making commodities like buttons:

> Some Negroes, and others, that can swim well and dive well, go naked into the water with a Knife in their Hand, and fight the Shark, and very commonly kill him, or wound him, so that he turns tail and runs away. Their Livors make good Oil to dress Leather withal; the Bones found in their Head are said to hasten Birth; and ease the Stone by bringing it away. Their Meat is eaten in scarce times, though I never could way with it, though a great Lover of Fish. Their backbone is of one entire thickness. Of the Bones or Joints I have known Buttons made, which serve well enough in Scarce Times and remote Places.[40]

Groups of slaves also went into the rivers and sounds to wrestle alligators to the shore, where others waited with axes to behead the giant creatures to entertain crowds of excited slaveholders. May, an African-born slave, reportedly leapt on the back of a harpooned manta ray and swam it back to the boat. A planter boastfully exclaimed, "Had he belonged to the Saxon or Norman race, he would have been knighted, and allowed to quarter on his shield the horns of the devil-fish, in token of his exploit!"[41]

Another area where slave boatmen from plantations had considerable educational value, leverage, and freedom was as plantation fishermen and hunters and even as crew aboard coastal vessels. A series of letters reminiscing about plantation life describes how, as a plantation child, Jones was accompanied by his childhood caretaker, a slave called "man Friday" or "boy Dick." The two were inseparable hunting and fishing companions. At an early age they were allowed only to set traps and to use "Indian implements" like bows and arrows. Later on Jones acquired a horse and was allowed to shoot bird shot—the "height of a country boy's ambition." They often made adventurous voyages in the rice fields in Jones's "bateau" with an "extemporized sail." The boat was provisioned with sweet potatoes to cook at a fire on shore. Jones describes how the "coffin-shaped" boat (probably a canoe) was built in the streets of "the quarters." The slaves joked that he might die in the so-called coffin. He delighted in going out in the boat to "churn" for fish in the low water with the "negro men and boys." The slave fishing crew knocked both ends out of a flour barrel and used it in a canal to capture fish by throwing it down, covering the barrels with their bodies, and grabbing the fish to throw to the younger boys, who had built a fish dam.[42]

When the rice fields dried up, alligators came out to eat the occasional pig or to grab the tail of a cow. A slave would wade into water up to his waist with a long slender pole to find the alligator and attach the pole under the alligator's foreleg. Once this was done, a tug of war ensued until the men dragged the alligator, "hissing like a goose," onto land. One single lethal blow with an axe severed the head and paralyzed the dangerous tail. Sometimes when the slaves could not find the alligators with the pole, they would come dangerously close to being bitten. The writer expounded romantically: "Master and servant preserved, shared the same sports, contributed to the familiar and affectionate relations which so notoriously from childhood bound master and servant together; and how it gave the Southern youth a skill with fire-arms rarely attained in the shooting gallery, and a free, firm and graceful seat in the saddle, seldom if ever acquired in the riding school; and how it developed a splendid physical manhood."[43]

A group of slaves identified as the "fishing Negroes" emerged in the Charleston area. A well-known fisherman, Moses, was often employed in net "knitting."[44] African fishermen traditionally made use of a variety of nets and were skilled in net casting and repairs. A surgeon, visiting the Gold Coast, wrote in his journal that it was "impossible to imagine how very dextrous the Negroes are in catching fish with a net."[45] An act establishing a separate fish market in Charleston acknowledged that "the business of fishing is principally carried on by Negroes, Mulattoes, and Mestizos." These fishermen were also able to exact whatever prices they wanted for their catch.[46] The independent character of slave fishermen clearly rested on access to and ownership of boats.[47] A local newspaper columnist observed that slaves dominated the fishing business because they were "permitted to keep boats, canows etc." The inventory of one Charleston home listed three slave fishermen but no boats belonging to their owner. This suggests that the slaves had their own boats or gained access to the sea as hired crew aboard a vessel belonging to someone else. Notices in newspapers for runaway slaves or advertisements include commentary describing a slave "who was possessed of a canoe."[48]

In addition to concerns about the independence of boatmen, fishing methods involving poisoning creeks, a practice found in West Africa and in the West Indies, became troublesome in the colony. Fishermen blocked off a creek, stream, or inlet and released mixtures composed of toxic plant substances and quicklime, causing fish to come to the surface. This practice became so prevalent that even South Carolina Assembly members raised concerns that "many persons in this Province do often use the pernicious practice of poisoning the creeks in order to catch a great quantity of fish."[49] Slaves also dammed tidal inlets with reed hedges or logs and caught fish using lines and wooden hooks. Faunal remains from archaeological sites reveal that common aquatic species that made up part of the diet of slaves included turtle, mullet, and top gaffsail fish.[50]

An entire class of "fishing Negroes emerged . . . replacing Native Americans as masters of the plentiful waters," a French visitor to the area remarked. During his visit to Charleston, he found himself "in the midst of twenty-five dugouts each containing four Negroes who were having excellent fishing, such as one might well desire on the eve of Good Friday."[51] The success of these black fishermen grew to such an extent that a special building was erected at the foot of Queen Street to serve as a fish market. Fishing was mainly inshore, and the dugout and periagua in various sizes served as the primary fishing craft. The English and French immigrants, while accustomed to hauling nets in oceangoing boats, were not at home in dugout canoes. In coping with the new environment, Africans drew not only upon their own experiences but also on their association with Native Americans.[52]

While slaves imparted their water survival skills to Europeans, they, in turn, were trained in European methods for constructing large ships. It is also likely that some slaves already had skills derived from African ship building or repair projects, although it is evident that shipwright colonists trained slaves to be proficient in European carpentry techniques. A notice in the *South Carolina Gazette* advertised "A fine Negro man, born in this country, brought up to the ship carpenters trade. "[53] Some boats were built and repaired on plantations by slaves, and shipwrights contracted with other slaves to do jobs in shipyards as temporary carpenters or as slaves owned and trained by the shipwrights themselves. Pierce Butler proudly described his plantation workforce to a prospective purchaser as including "carpenters [that] require no White man to enable them to erect a good House as I desire to occupy. They glaze also. My ship carpenters have built me two Sea Vessels without any white person directing them."[54] The Historian Mary Carrill examined the role played by black artisans, including hired-out plantation slaves who worked as carpenters or boatbuilders in the South.[55] The shortest time for hiring out a slave carpenter was one year, and the longest time was eight years. On average a slave worked as an artisan for around four years. The majority of artisans hired out by planters in the Charleston area were under the age of thirty. Slaves had considerable versatility in their roles as carpenter. For example, artisans might be listed as "house and ship carpenter," "jobbing carpenter and boatman," "sawyer and shipwright," or "sawyer and boatman."[56] Native American slaves, like African slaves, were employed in urban and technical crafts. This is supported by advertisements in newspapers that list a runaway from Roger Saunders: "An Indian man named Peter, he was a carpenter and a wheelwright."[57]

African shipwrights in Charleston were usually hired from plantations at twenty pounds a month in local currency. At least thirteen of the twenty South Carolina shipwrights in the 1730s and 1740s used slave carpenters. The market value of the purchase of shipyard slaves was determined by their shipyard skill and generally ranged between £300 and £800 depending on the slave's specific skill or experience (in contrast, a field hand was worth about £60). For example, caulkers were valued between £300 and £350 pounds because their trade was easier to learn and thus less valuable. Trained slave shipwrights were the most valued. Notices in the *South Carolina Gazette* reveal that Robin, trained by the shipbuilder John Daniel, was valued at £450. The large number of slaves in the colony and their high value when trained resulted in a heavy investment by South Carolinians in slave shipwrights, who were involved in the actual construction rather than performing tasks such as caulking and painting. This trend especially influenced the social dynamics of shipbuilding in Charleston.[58]

The wages of a free shipwright in South Carolina were a third greater than those of a slave. This contrasted with New England, where slave owners charged the same for slaves and for European labor. In 1744, shipbuilders, represented by Andrew Ruck of Charleston, who did not own slaves, petitioned the Commons House of Assembly to curtail the employment of shipyard slaves employed "in mending, repairing and caulking of Ships and other Vessels and Boats, and working at the Shipwrights Trade and Business in this Town." The petitioners claimed that free white shipwrights who "had served their Times to the Trade of Shipwright, could meet with little or no Work to do, and that themselves and their families were reduced to Poverty." They simply could not compete with the cheap labor provided by slaves. The planters who hired out slaves and the shipwrights who used them argued in response that it was their hard work and savings that had allowed them the opportunity to hire them. Moreover, they claimed that the existing system allowed them to support slave families when "by Age or Infirmity they became incapable of Labor." They countered the charge of that they were responsible for the lack of employment for white shipyard workers by citing examples where these shipwrights simply did not respond to urgent labor solicitations by ship owners in a timely manner, causing them to use slave labor. Neither did they understand why shipwrights expected to be instantly employed upon the day of arrival in South Carolina, as this was not the case in any other trade.[59]

A Committee of the Commons House recommended that a limitation be placed on the number of slaves hired out by planters as shipwrights. In 1751 the South Carolina Assembly placed taxes on the import of slaves and designated a fifth of the revenue from the tax to be used as a bounty to encourage shipwrights and other maritime-related laborers to settle in South Carolina. After this ruling, the shipbuilding industry started to thrive, and European shipwrights flocked to the area. The Assembly appointed a committee to investigate the contentious issue. In attempting to find a compromise between slave and free labor, the committee reached no real conclusion, a result unsatisfactory to both parties. Through the years there were repeated requests for the protection of white shipwrights that the legislature simply evaded, not wanting to give either group and economic advantage, and the idea was finally abandoned. By the 1760s, the use of slaves in the shipyards of Charleston was widespread, some hired from plantations and others purchased by the shipwrights as they became more established in their businesses.[60]

The economic value placed on slaves with specific skills either brought from Africa or learned in Carolina began to create tensions and frustration among whites seeking employment in those professions. Petitions from European-born laborers for relief from slave competition were strongly countered by slave owners—either planters or shipwrights—who felt they had every right to use and to train their slaves in work skills as they saw fit. Historians suggest that the institution of slavery, buttressed by the dominant planter aristocracy, permeated the city of Charleston, which they characterize as an agriculture-dependent colony with economic links to Britain closer than those of any other eastern seaport. Urban slavery had a devastating impact on white artisans and tradesmen and was a critical factor in Charleston's demise as a major commercial center in the nineteenth century. It presented an unattractive labor market for white workers and checked the growth of the middle class.[61]

In contrast, a black artisan group composed of hired or owned slaves began to emerge.[62] Compared to other East Coast seaports like New York, Boston, and Philadelphia, the Charleston slave population increased after 1750.[63]

The Material Culture Record: Plantation Boat Museum Exhibits

Given Charleston's multicultural heritage, derived from its French Huguenots, Angolan slaves who spoke Portuguese, and early Spanish explorers, it is not surprising that the term "piragua" became commonly used to denote a boat form. Some maritime historians believe the meaning is restricted to a dugout canoe base with a plank added or to a multilog dugout as described in the southeastern records. This book finds, however, that the term had greater flexibility in usage and that its meaning may have changed over time to include variations on the basic boat design. From the context of the literature of the colonial period, it appears that the vessel type "pirogue" was a boat used by the coastal militia and for river and shoreline work but not in the intercolonial West Indies or European trade.

The crew of these periaguas were most often composed of slave boatmen under the supervision of either a slave or white patroon who was employed by the planter or by a white scout boat captain with his mixed-race militia (both Native American and African). These vernacular boats were not restricted to having a specific type of hull design, boat size, tonnage, or rig. One can assume from the many newspaper advertisements listing their tonnage that by the mid-1700s the term was not used for very large vessels. There was a high probability

Figure 12. Fishing vessel, ca. early to mid-1900s. Used by permission of the Charleston Museum.

that such a boat would be either a sloop or schooner rig with masts that were movable for bridges, perhaps a single-log or split-log design, or a variation of the flat-bottomed ship-built design, with a hull shape and draft that varied depending on individual owners' needs for loading at his property and the extent of the river or shoreline work for which the owner intended to use the particular vessel.

Although most plantation boats referred to as periaguas are underwater or embedded in riverbanks, there are a few examples of plantation boats, some in museums. The *Bessie,* exhibited in the Charleston Museum courtyard, is often used to train archaeology students in recording techniques. It was owned by General Arthur Middleton Manigault at White Oak Plantation on the North Santee River. The giant canoe measures twenty-nine feet six inches long and five feet ten inches wide. The boat or periagua has a plumb bow and wine glass transom, suggesting that it was versatile enough for use at sea or along the coast. Other features include half frames and thwart knees of live oak, two mast steps, and a large centerboard trunk.

Figure 13. Plantation boat Bessie *at the Charleston Museum. Photo by Lynn Harris, permission of the Charleston Museum.*

Figure 14. Plantation boat Accommodation. Used by permission of Maritime Studies East Carolina University.

The *Accommodation,* previously stored in a warehouse on Dill Plantation and now at Middleton Plantation, had a hull built of two logs joined in the center by a keelson, with rising strakes added to the gunwales to raise the freeboard. It has a length of twenty-eight feet two inches and a beam of five feet. Twenty-three small framing and floor members one to two inches in thickness run along the length of the vessel. Seven seating thwarts are located approximately two feet seven inches apart. The second seat from the bow has a hole in the middle, which may have been utilized for a removable mast, awning pole, or cargo-loading boom. Extra strakes were added above the logs to increase the freeboard. The name of the owner, "Hinson," was stenciled into the transom. Museum paperwork shows that the *Accommodation* was used on the Waccamaw River and was purchased by Mr. Hinson in 1855 for $150.[64]

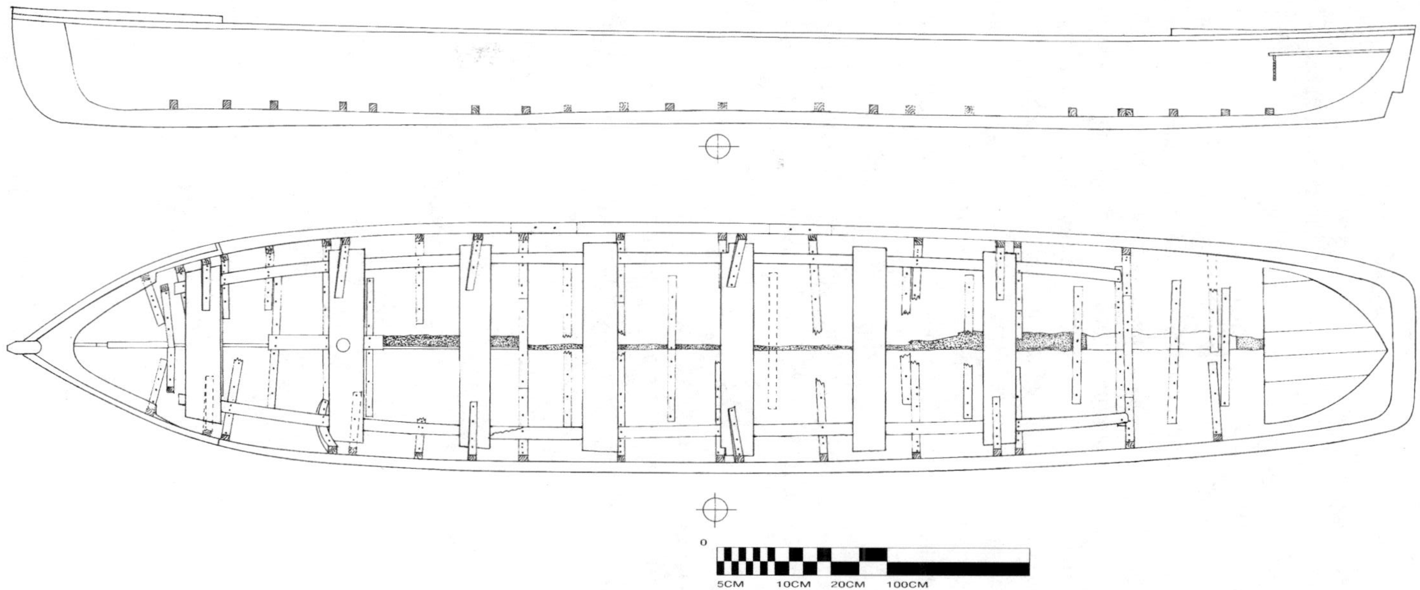

Figure 15. Plan view of the Accomodation. Used by permission of Maritime Studies East Carolina University.

6.

Fair Winds, Fair Trade, and Fair Due

Trade networks orchestrated by plantation patroons and their slave crew proliferated in the late 1700s and the early decades of the 1800s. In 1796 the General Assembly passed "An Act more effectually to Prevent Shopkeepers, Traders and Others, from dealing with Slaves having no Tickets from their Owners." Anyone who traded corn, rice, peas, flour, bacon, tobacco, cotton, or indigo with slaves would be fined $200. By 1817 this increased to $1,000, and those who violated the law also faced a possible prison sentence of up to one year. Slave owners faced a challenging dilemma. They had to confront and regulate secret trading among slaves, free blacks, and whites. Often this trading served to benefit the plantation owners and was considered an unspoken private and internal domestic arrangement with the planter who owned the slaves. It was their prerogative whether to allow the slaves to trade. Despite numerous efforts to control the slave trade, it was impossible to do this effectively.[1]

There was ample opportunity for illegal trade as commerce flourished in the port city. The *South Carolina Gazette* announced ships seeking cargo and selling merchandise: "For Portugal, Spain, or any Port in Great Britain, and a MARKET—the ship JOHN AND BETSY, burthen 850 barrels for freight, apply to master"; "For JAMAICA—the Brigantine HARRIOT, for freight apply to Master. A few hogsheads of exceeding good Jamaica Rum, fine Muscovada Sugar to be sold reasonably";[2] and "For PHILADELPHIA—the Scooner POLLY—for freight or passage apply to the said master at Motte's Wharf. Who has to sell at any store on said wharf choice RUM, BEER, CYDER, and some very good HEMP SEED."[3]

Coastal, West Indies, and European shipping trade to and from the port city of Charleston had become a lively and lucrative business operation by the late eighteenth century, and the waterfront bustled with activity. East Bay Street, running alongside the Cooper River, was speckled with wharves piled high with rice barrels and ships waiting to load and unload cargoes. Hotels, mansions, warehouses, stores, and public houses lined the waterfront, the latter frequented by raucous sailors and fishermen telling tales and making sales.

Merchants meandered in and out of the Customs House building to settle bonds, collect their mail, and shop at the variety of stores or at the outdoor markets where black women hawked their fish, meat, and vegetables. In addition to serving aboard vessels, both male and female slaves became intricately involved in the Charleston port market. They served and self-hired themselves as factors, agents, and operators of water taxis. They transported stolen goods and legal goods, including meat, vegetables, corn, rice, whiskey, rum, gin, and wine, on boats along the river systems to Charleston. Slave owners allowed slaves additional privileges as patroons and market profiteers. Others lost money and complained bitterly about the freedoms slaves were allowed and about slaves who took advantage of the situation to smuggle goods in a "black market." Written permits allowed slaves and free persons of color to transport these goods from one section of the city to another, but businessmen claimed that often these permits were forged "in the name of a fictitious person."[4]

Increased oceanic trade meant an increased need for riverboats and riverboat crew to transport cargoes along the inland waterways to the Charleston port. Riverboat traffic was tuned to the seasonal rhythm of ocean trade. Boatmen, usually engaged in river work, were employed or hired out by planters as seamen and as workers in urban shipyards. Country factors, ferry operators, and wharf owners saw advantages in owning crews of riverboat slaves, too. Ongoing tensions with local and empire agents reached a peak in these years, most evident in the planters' negative reactions to boating regulations along the rivers and coastline. These tensions laid the seeds of unrest the helped lead to the American Revolution.

The social hierarchy and work opportunities within the colony were changing. It was a population composed of a powerful plantocracy, skilled immigrant artisans, and a cheap and convenient plantation slave labor force. Along the city shoreline African slaves mingled with Scotsmen, Irishmen, Frenchmen, and Englishmen on streets, in markets, or in workshops. They worked side by side as laborers, apprentices, craftsmen, plantation boatmen, or seamen aboard coasting schooners or West Indies sloops. By this time, vessels voyaged up and down the Georgia, South Carolina, and Florida coastline and to the West Indies almost continually. Others ventured from Charleston across the Atlantic to trade in a multitude of European markets. One of the most important British markets was Bristol, whose ships supplied Charleston with wine from Tenerife or Cadiz, slaves from West Africa, and occasionally fish from New England and

Newfoundland. They returned to their home port with cargoes of rice, tar, pitch, indigo, timber, and skins. Some sailed from Charleston to Hamburg and then to Stockholm, returning to Bristol via a roundabout way. It was not a simple two-way return route but a complex radiating trading voyage.[5]

Governor William Bull of South Carolina reported to Britain that "within the last three months 360 sails from different countries arrived in Charleston."[6] He boasted that the "quantity of rice is 111,310 barrels and indigo 545,620 weight" for the successful colony, where he had the "satisfaction to acquaint your Lordships that no illicit trade is being carried out in this province or a suspicion of any sort of practices."[7] The rhythm of shipping in Charleston was linked to the agricultural seasons. In October, when harvests peaked and cold weather killed the fever-carrying mosquitoes, plantation boats flocked down the rivers to the city docks. River shipping was delayed if there were droughts and therefore not enough water to fill the streams. Once the rivers and creeks were navigable, plantation commerce bustled through to December. From January to April oceangoing ships thronged the harbor with their captains competing aggressively for freights. If ships intended to make two round trips between Charleston and Europe, they had to leave by mid-January and be back by mid-April for a second cargo. During these frenetic months business and profit were foremost in the minds of planters, merchants, and sea captains. Plantation boatmen plied the waterways conducting assorted tasks.

Entries in the ledger belonging to the Ball family on the Cooper River list how slave boatmen "Salisbury and Amos went town by water" to work for another family member. On another occasion Salisbury took a Mrs. Doggett to town "by water" and to fetch "21 cord of wood." Sometimes boatmen were hired out to work for other planters or businessmen in need of extra transportation. The boatman's time was obviously valuable, and his tasks varied. A list of goods sold to "Mr Thomas, the Periauger man" suggests that owning, operating, building, and repairing plantation boats had become an increasingly serious business venture. The hours, days, or weeks that a carpenter spent working or took off were carefully noted in the business accounting records, revealing that employers were intimately aware of the importance of managing their laborers' time.[8]

A February 10, 1785, entry by Charles Drayton in his diary mentions a plantation "pettiauger" that was a sloop named *Wadmalaw.* The boat carried supplies for building at Drayton Hall and barrels of rice.[9] He also mentions, on July 4, 1784, a "flat" belonging to "AM" (Arthur Middleton) that carried barrels of corn and, on January 2, 1807, a schooner that carried a load of sixty-nine barrels of rice and three bales of cotton from Drayton Hall to Charleston. In January 1808 he mentioned that the schooner had arrived at Mr. Laurens's wharf, where she sank and the bushels of rice got wet. In February 1808 he wrote that twelve canoes were used to carry turkeys to Charleston.

By June, the harbor traffic returned to a more languid pace. Coastal packets and ships loaded with rice for the Caribbean trade dotted the waters of the slow-moving port until September. As a Charleston merchant, Robert Pringle, declared, "we have little or no Trade in the hot Season of June, July and August & there is no good Rice of the Crop left fit to Ship to Europe to be purchas'd."[10] The oppressive summer heat and the unhealthy climate gave merchants and planters time to undertake business or pleasure trips to the northern colonies or to Europe.[11] Those ships that did not manage to obtain full cargoes waited until the next season. Instead of paying wharfage fees, they anchored at an inland river venue, one of which was Childesbury on the West Branch of the Cooper River. Pringle describes how "all the Vessels are hurrying to gett away, & we shall have few Remaining here, excepting what Lye up Cooper River at Childesbury where there is already Eight or Ten Sail that Lye till next Crop."[12]

Healthy trade meant that there was a need for more ships to be built and repaired, for more crew, and for increased provisions for longer voyages. Toward the end of the 1700s Charleston harbor had "upward of 130 boats and schooners and three-fourths of them decked, carrying 10–50 tons at four barrels of rice to the ton employed in bringing in country produce."[13] Carolinians employed a variety of vessels at this time. These included inland boats of a few tons' burden, which carried on the interior trade of the colony because larger vessels would have grounded on the shoals of rivers. Many of these were undecked. The largest of these river vessels had trunk masts that had to be folded when they passed under a bridge. Coasters that drew too much water to be used inland (described as "decked periuagers") were generally fifty-ton burden and collected produce from the plantation landings and the depots of port towns.[14] Waterfront sketches of Charleston and the Cooper River show a variety of boats, including three-masted ships (barques or fluyts), single-masted sloops or periaguas, and a variety of smaller rowboats and canoes.[15]

Local newspaper listings of boats lost, built, launched, and for sale provide a good indication of the types of vessels used and built in South Carolina at the time. The *South Carolina Gazette* often carried announcements like these: "a new Scooner lately launched about 130 or 140 barrels, (not yet fitted with sails) being too large for the person she was built. She is estimated to be a compleat (for the coasting trade) as well as any built in this province,"[16] "for sale: a very valuable Scooner, burthen 30 tons, draws 5 feet and 6 inches of water when loaded";[17] "for sale: a Scooner Sally, Carolina built, burthern about two hundred barrels of rice . . . as small draught of water as most schooners that carry no more than 150 barrels, and a remarkable fast sailer, is well calculated for the West India and the coasting business. The vessel is sold for no other reason than she cannot go up many of the little creeks the owner intended she should."[18] The notices reveal that adaptations that suited boats' design to the local environment, especially the shallow rivers, were important considerations. Speed and cargo space were design assets for ships involved in the West Indies and coastal trade, where there was a danger of piracy and speed was important to ensure that cargoes reached their destinations in a timely manner.

Some notices provide the finer details of ship construction, such as the description of the schooner *Betsy,* a pilot boat belonging to William Kelly, that had a "length of keel, 27 ½ feet, strait rabbit, 11 feet beam or better, a shallow square tuck about 13 inches deep, the head of the stern post before the rudder café in the cockpit is cedar, . . . the new mainmast of this country pine, the foremast a Northward spruce pine, the bowsprit the country pine, with a great many worm holes in it, her boot-tops are painted with white lead and oil, her bends black, sides yellow, counter red, quarters and stern green, timber heads and crutches vermillion red, and inside Spanish brown."[19]

The majority of registered sailboats in South Carolina waters were schooners (two masts), considered to be more weatherly and suitable for the fluctuating wind conditions of the rivers and coastal trade. Small schooners had two masts, which were usually fore- and aft-rigged. Larger vessels of the rig may have been rigged more like brigantines, another popular class of colonial vessel, with square sails on the fore mast and fore and aft sails on the main mast.[20] A schooner rig placed the masts away from the center of the boat, creating a central cargo area free of obstructions; this arrangement was suited to long, narrow craft because a large amount of sail area could be divided between the two masts and handled more easily by a smaller crew. Boats without high masts may have had advantage when it was necessary to pass under bridges or take down a mast.[21]

Sloops of this time period seem to have carried a fairly consistent rig of fore and aft and square sails. In the former category were mainsail, foresail or, as we term them today, staysail, jib, and flying jib. Square sail arrangements included a topsail and sometimes a topgallant, while sloops used in the bays and rivers, where tacking was necessary, did not have square sails. Fore and aft mainsails were fitted with booms and had short gaffs, which became longer by the 1800s. Mainsails were boomless and furled by brailling into the mast.[22]

South Carolina ship registration records display some interesting trends. South Carolina had fewer sloops and more schooners than New York. Carolina sloops were built to an equal tonnage and could carry as much cargo as the New York sloops. South Carolina registered vessels classified as ships, brigs, and snows had a greater tonnage than those in New York colony and were most likely bulk cargo carriers designed to carry heavy loads of staple crops such as rice. South Carolina's schooners, the most popular rig type, had less tonnage than their New York counterparts.[23] This may be attributed to the need to be fast, small, easy to handle, and easy to hide in an era of illicit trade and smuggling.

Boats bound for the European market usually carried the cargoes of more than one planter in order to fill the hold. These cooperative business agreements did have the potential to cause problems between partners. Henry Laurens complained to the merchant Charles Crokatt that upon two occasions he had became involved in disputes with buyers in the English Channel about the quality of his rice. Knowing that his rice was of the very best quality, he "made a general resolution never to Ship rice for a foreign market but in Vessels Loaden wholly by myself or in conjunction with some friend upon whose attention to the quality of his goods I could depend."[24] Shipwrights designed vessels with dimensions or scantlings to accommodate a required number of rice barrels, because without a full cargo an ocean crossing was simply not a lucrative enterprise.

In a letter advising Richard Oswald, Laurens relayed the comments of an experienced shipwright, John Rose, who was building a ship for Oswald's intended rice trade.[25] Although Oswald sent specifications for the vessel's design to Charleston, John Rose argued that the measurements, especially the narrow beam and the shallow depth of hold, were impractical for the carrying trade. Ideally the depth of hold should be nine feet nine inches to accommodate three tiers of barrels for rice. This would also be a good dimension for the sugar trade from the Windward Islands. The beam for a vessel like this should be at least twenty feet six inches or twenty-one feet.[26]

Governor James Glen of South Carolina gave further insights into restrictions of boat design determined by the characteristics of waterways and estuaries by elaborating:

> South Carolina hath Seventy Leagues of Sea Coast reckoning from Cape Fear northward, to the River May southward. . . . That River [Port Royal] hath Depth of Water enough for any Ship in the World, in or out, and as good a Harbour as any that Nature hath made . . . the next River is Edisto, a good River for Ships and Vessels not drawing above Twelve feet of Water. North Edisto is equally good, and hath a clear Harbour Entrance. Stone Harbour is not a Harbour for any Vessel not drawing about Eleven Feet Water. . . . Charleston Harbour is fit for all Vessels which do not exceed fifteen feet Draught. Sewee and Santee Rivers are for Small Craft not drawing more than eight or nine feet. Into the Port of Winyaw there is a channel Twelve Feet Deep. . . . Cape Fear River, alias Clarendon River, the reputed Boundary between North and South Carolina is a very fine bold River for any ship in fair weather, or at any other time, for ships not exceeding Fifteen

or Sixteen Feet Draught, there are not less than three Fathom deep at low water in the worst part of the channel.[27]

Descriptions of waterways show clearly that certain rivers did not permit navigation by deep-draught vessels, supporting the notion that either auxiliary small craft were a necessity or ships had to be built with a draught suited to entering a particular harbor or negotiating a particular river. This was clearly taken into account by planters and country factors who relied heavily on an economy tied to inland boating. Heavy boat traffic up and down inland waterways, often too shallow for navigation, created a need for country factors, who provided essential accessories wharves or spaces on wharves with stores where country produce could be exchanged. For example, John Morley, a country factor, had spacious stores on Colonel Beale's wharf where he combined businesses in indigo, rice, and lumber with carting and selling wood.[28] Morley interacted with planters and found it profitable to employ their slaves in cutting and transporting wood to wharfside stores operated by factors. Country factors themselves owned boat slaves. John Morley had two schooners for his business: *Anne and Martha,* with a carrying capacity of 110 barrels of rice, and *Cannon Brothers,* with a carrying capacity of 150 barrels of rice. He also had 130 to 140 slaves working for him, including twelve boatmen and three patroons.[29]

Merchants charged planters for transportation services such as the use of their ferry landings and ferries. The Strawberry Ferry Ledger of Lancelot Smith, covering the period from 1777 to 1779, contains a two-page account for Henry Laurens. The ferry crossed the Western Branch of the Cooper River about two miles below his plantation, Mepkin, at the town of Childesbury. The charges itemize the fees charged, including that for one trip across the river carrying "2 boys and a horse, 3 Negroes and 3 horses, a Cart of Mr. Izards and Oxen, or a Coach, 3 chairs and a horse."[30]

Similarly, in the port city of Charleston, the expense of wharfage, porterage, and stowage became increasingly important considerations for planters with boats or shares in ships. The ledger of Henry Laurens attested to these regular expenditures.[31] It lists running costs for sundry wharfage and other accompanying services, such as like porterage—loading and unloading boat cargoes. Merchants and planters regarded retailers who did business like this on a petty scale as occupying a lower social and economic niche with aspirations toward plantation ownership. Henry Laurens wrote in a letter that country factors were "no planters—easily perceived they have understanding and industry enough to make very good ones in a short time with the assistance of a capable overseer for one or two years and once they are set down in a creditable manner as planters, they may carry on the Sale of many specie of European and West Indian goods to some advantage & with good grace."[32] Although patronizing in tone, this remark does reveal that, with the appropriate guidance, upward mobility was possible for the retailer with aspirations toward planter status.

As when they served aboard boats, slaves both helped and hindered wharf work on rivers and in the seaport. They disregarded the slave code, often taking temporary illegal jobs as stevedores, boat hands, messengers, carpenters, and day laborers. They were available at shorter notice and for lower pay than European workers. This worked well for employers who did not have to make up contracts with the slave's owners, allowing a flexible and immediate labor supply.[33] Both planters and factors preferred owning "seasoned" slaves with skills that were useful to their business enterprises. These slaves were considered more valuable and reliable than slaves directly out of Africa. A similar preference was exercised in selecting urban slaves. During the latter part of the 1760s, newspapers were filled with advertisements for skilled slaves, especially boatmen, sawyers, and coopers. Notices in the *South Carolina Gazette* describe "upward of one hundred Negroes among whom are many valuable tradesmen on the Ashley River." Slaves were employed in almost every branch of business, generating much wealth for the owners of skilled slaves both in the southern colonies and in the West Indies. At the same time, "new" slaves brought from Africa in large shiploads were being purchased, and planters used seasoned slaves to teach them skills, including the English language and aspects of plantation work. A planter wrote that "the Governor does not understand Plantation affairs so well as some of us Southern Folks." He continued later that the "tasks that valuable seasoned plantation slaves could perform new or Ship'd Negroes cannot perform."[34]

While designated patroons most often were seasoned, reliable slaves, it appears that the new, troublesome arrivals were placed on boats under the direct and controlled supervision of a white patroon. Two new slaves, recently purchased, who ran away from Wambaw Plantation were captured and sent back on the plantation boat with the recommendation that either both should be sold or one used as a boat slave aboard the Schooner *Thomas*, under strict supervision.[35] Boatmen, with their relative freedoms and their growing confidence, became increasingly important sources of information about the larger cultural landscape of the Atlantic world beyond the plantation. Placing headstrong and disruptive slaves aboard boats served to create social distances between field slaves but was also a gamble and a dangerous choice. Planters considered boat slaves an integral part of the overall value of a boat, almost an accessory. Henry Laurens's ledger lists the value of the schooner *Baker* and "4 Negroes on board her" as £2,600 and the value of plantation schooner *Wambaw* and the "5 Negroes on board her" as £3,200.[36]

Revolutionary War unrest among the Charleston community may also have contributed to the freedom and desertion rate of boatmen. For example, a "stout Negro" named Shadwell from John Alleyne Walter's schooner deserted at

Lamboll's Bridge on November 21, 1775. Walters claimed that he was well acquainted with all the rivers and inlets south of Charleston. Slaves like Shadwell, along with the boatmen in his crew, had considerable time without white supervision and often enjoyed an independent income from petty trading along their inland boating route and at the port markets.[37] All around the colony people began to remark on the integral role that slaves played within the internal economy. A planter on the Santee River commented that "patroons of Schooners and other small Craft were allowed (as they pass and repass up and down our river) to Trade, Traffick, Barter, and Sell to and with the Negroe slaves, to the great Prejudice of their Owners." On the Combahee River rice planters complained that "peddling [*sic*] boats which frequent the river, who want only a public landing, as a station to enable them to remain in the vicinity of the large and productive rice plantations, for the purpose of trading with the Negroe Slaves, to the very great loss of the Owners, and Corruption of such Slaves."[38]

Charles Ball, a slave, wrote an autobiography describing whites' willingness to participate in this illicit trade. He was put in charge of laying seine nets from his canoe to fish for shad. When he observed a large sailing boat captained by a white person docking on the river, he took advantage of the situation by trading one hundred pounds of bacon for three hundred pounds of shad. The captain told him in a low voice that he would be down the river again in two weeks and that he would be glad to buy more produce, adding, "I will give you half as much for the cotton as it is worth in Charleston, and pay you either in money or groceries as you choose. Take care and do not betray yourself, and I shall be honest with you."[39]

It is estimated that by 1782 46 percent of slave mariners in South Carolina were listed as sailors as opposed to boatmen and fishermen. With an increase in the volume of coastal and ocean trade and greater participation by local planters and merchants in the economy, undoubtedly more slaves discovered their sea legs. African Americans now crossed oceans or sailed extensively.[40] Robert Pringle, a merchant, experienced frequent business delays caused by a shortage of seamen. One of his vessels was "detained for sometime for want of hands," and he complained that "Seamen are so very Scarce & Difficult to obtain here."[41] Slave mariners or laborers helped to alleviate this problem. Slave crews hired by seagoing boats were moneymakers for planters. Costs of £350 each for the services of two sailors—Jack on the ship *Flora* and Topaz on the sloop *Henry*—are listed in a Charleston plantation ledger.[42] John Evans, master of the Brigantine *Dolphin*, was helped by a crew of "four stout Negro men" sent to him via Robert Pringle to "to assist you on board & who are Used to be upon the Water & Understand to work on Shipboard."[43] In the West Indies, too, black seamen proliferated both before and after the Revolution. Similar to the pattern of events in shipyards, in the years before the Revolution the presence of large numbers of skilled black seamen began to jeopardize opportunities for the whites who sought employment and higher wages.[44]

In contrast to some other ports, Charleston had a vice admiralty court where white seamen could bring claims collectively against their masters by suing as a group. Most important, Judges Nicholas Trott, William Blakely, and Maurice Lewis sometimes issued rulings in favor of the seamen. This was a threat to planters and merchants alike who owned or co-owned ships. Seamen were scarce enough in Charleston, and it was easy for them to desert, sue, or find another return boat to Europe. Desertion was a major problem and caused work stoppages and thus financial losses to ship owners. Mutinous crews were yet another problem.[45]

Sending troublesome slave riverboatmen to sea may also have helped both planters and merchants to acquire a more subservient workforce, one that they could control more easily than European sailors, who were often considered the dregs of society. This was a period of naval impressments and offered a solution to the problem of the white "rabble" in port cities. Those who left land willingly were usually in flight, outcasts, deserters, bail-jumpers, thieves, murderers, in trouble with the law, or men with little hope of success in a life on shore. Laws governing seamen were paternalistic. The purpose was to supply a cheap, docile labor supply. Seamen were treated like slaves, seen as childlike dependents, yet they required wages. There were laws allowing the whipping disobedient seamen; laws prohibiting seamen from leaving their vessels after sundown or traveling on land without certificates; laws against extending credit to seamen; laws against selling liquor to them; laws waiving imprisonment for seamen convicted of cursing; and laws requiring masters to give discharge certificates to crew members so that they could be rehired. Benevolent laws required that seamen receive a good diet and accommodations, and there were punishments for masters who maimed, beat, or wounded their crews.[46]

Thus, sending a bonded African plantation boat man to sea may not have been a promotion from a riverboat but rather a control mechanism and a way to solve the problems of labor scarcity, desertion, mutiny, and the need to pay high wages to scarce and troublesome white crews. How much freedom did these enslaved seamen actually have compared to those patroons who roamed the rivers and port cities? How did the rebellious shipboard slaves, barred from plantation boats, interact with the white reprobates? White seaman may have resented being in the same boat as slave seamen, both literally and figuratively. Again, this situation was not always clear-cut. Perhaps the seamen found some common ground in their mutual plights as subservient seagoing laborers and even bonded within the context of their situation. Evidence of multiracial mobs under the leadership of seamen in port cities, including Charleston, is testimony to the seamen's perception of a common identity and plight that crossed the color line by the 1770s.

In December 1775 the South Carolina Council of Safety complained about attacks by sailors, both "white and black armed men."[47] The same year Thomas Jeremiah, a riverboat pilot, was arrested for stockpiling guns as he waited for the war that would "help the poor Negroes." Two or three white sailors were also held under suspicion as part of the plot but were later released for lack of evidence.[48] A smaller percentage of white seamen were not the bail jumpers and victims of impressments but rather young men who went to sea to appease their adventurous spirit, saw the world, eventually became masters, and earned high wages that allowed them to retire on land at an early age. For most of these young men, their relationships with slaves on board ships were simply an extension of the relationships they had with enslaved watermen on land.

During this era shipping became an investment not only for merchants and planters as it had been in previous decades but also for successful artisans. Merchants Benjamin Hawes and George Flagg bought a fifteen-ton vessel for the coastal and West Indian trade. Others, like Walter Mansell, a tailor, Nathaniel Lebby, a coachmaker, and George Sheed, a ship plumber, formed a partnership and together purchased a sixty-five-ton vessel. Shipwrights, too, like John Rose and Thomas Cochrane, joined the carrying trade.[49] The growth of trade and shipbuilding in the rapidly maturing colony escalated tensions between British authorities and local colonial officials. The government had to recoup losses incurred during the Seven Years' War, a national debt of £148 million pounds, and other losses from smuggling, especially in the northern colonies. There were two remedies to this situation: increased tax collection and laws to prevent smuggling. Governor James Glen wrote a damning letter composed of detailed observations on the plantation trade and the Navigation Acts, which alerted British officials, who cast wary eyes at Charleston. He wrote that the local coastline extended for 150 miles, interrupted by rivers, creeks, and inlets where vessels could "unload at pleasure without great Risque of being disturbed, in like manner they may load enumerated goods, or such as are prohibited for export, or carry them to foreign ports, besides as our produce is most bulky most Planters keep large decked boats." He elaborated that although these plantation boats were kept as coasters, they were capable of performing foreign voyages as they were not regulated by any office. Although Governor Glen claimed that he had been assured that there was little illegal trade in South Carolina, he qualified this statement by admitting that this was in comparison to the scale of such trade in other colonial provinces and that he was subsequently "convinced and [knew] for certain there is very considerable illegal trade in this province, injurious to the Fair Trader, highly hurtful to the King's Revenue, and Destructive to the Manufactures of Britain."[50]

A new kind of hybrid dual-use inland/coastal plantation boat evolved as the growing community began to break its dependency on Europe. There were often differences in opinion concerning the law, and doubts arose as to what constituted a "decked seagoing" vessel. Breaches of the Navigation Acts occurred frequently in the unwatched rivers and sounds. Plantation boats ran goods on their own account or acted in collusion with larger vessels lying in deeper waters. Under the cover of night they landed and loaded barrels and bales onto ships or into secret hiding places along the shoreline. As part of a class of vessels that did not require formal registration, smaller in size although seaworthy, they had much more leeway in illegal trading activities.[51]

Article 1043, "Exportation of Enumerated Commodities," on trade instructions enacted for the colonies, lists taxation according to vessel size. The lower-tonnage range may reflect frugality to save the expenses of a larger vessel. A smaller ship required fewer crew, paid lower port dues, and, most significant, required a smaller bond to be paid to customs officers (a bond of £1,000 was attached to a vessel of less than one hundred tons, whereas a bond of £2,000 was required for a vessel of more than one hundred tons). Increasing size was similar to moving into the next tax bracket.[52]

Under Governor Thomas Boone's administration, the South Carolina legislature required plantation vessels conducting intercolonial trade within South Carolina waters to acquire an annual bond from a local official.[53] If coasting schooners and plantation periagoes did not carry rice out of the colony, they would not be required to clear customs, as were ships bound for other parts of the king's dominion. Officials became increasingly vigilant in enforcing these regulations in a manner in which the planters and merchants considered to be unfair, odious, and inordinately officious. Planter correspondence during this decade is filled with complaints about Customs House officials. They described them as "rapacious, haughty, insolent, overbearing, and wicked." The King, one planter wrote, "never had in this province so vile a set of servants in the custom house as there are at present."[54] The situation was so bad that "these wicked officials had alienated the affections of the Americans from the Mother Country even more than the Laws so complained of by the Americans."[55]

On March 28, 1765, Governor William Bull wrote to the Commissioners of Trade and Plantations that he wanted to bring to their notice "a hardship to which the coasting trade and consequently the General Marine Trade of the Province is exposed to and threatened with seizures under the pretext of the Navigation Acts from which it has hitherto been free."[56] He described how naval officers were empowered by the Commissioners of Customs to seize and take bonded and decked (necessary to protect cargoes from the weather) plantation periagoes carrying rice and indigo cargoes and to haul their owners into Admiralty Court. Although riverboats were simply passing along this part of the coastline to avoid sections of the river that were too shallow, the customs officials charged the captains of the plantation boats with not having the official paperwork and with neglecting to clear their vessels through customs houses, as if the boats were conducting coastal or oceanic trade.

Two years after William Bull made the complaint, Henry Laurens's vessel the schooner *Wambaw* of fifteen tons' burden, bound from Charleston to his Altamaha property in Georgia, was seized by George Roupell, the Searcher of Customs, on its return to the port city.[57] James Baillie, his overseer at Broughton Island, apparently checked the accounts for Henry Laurens. The account included rice, beef, and a swivel gun, in addition to the hire of a periogoe and a flatt or barge. The *Wambaw* was carrying plantation goods, such as tools and provisions, rather than enumerated trade items. It had not left South Carolina waters. Nonetheless, the ship was accused of not clearing custom before leaving for Georgia.[58]

Laurens ultimately turned to the Court of Common Pleas to seek damages from Roupell for what he perceived as the illegal seizure of his boats and spearheaded a movement in the merchant community to get rid of Daniel Moore, the English Collector of Customs. These actions prompted escalating events and tensions between the British government and Charleston merchants. The controversy over customs regulations and enforcement actions involving his plantation boats clearly propelled Henry Laurens and his many supporters away from their loyalties to the Crown and moved them into the rebel camp. It was also conceivably a turning point in the mindset of many affluent and influential Carolinians connected socially to the illustrious Henry Laurens with regard to the approaching American Revolution.[59]

Questions arise about whether shipping regulations were a tool used arbitrarily by the English government or local officials to regulate important and wealthy leaders in the community whose business was intricately linked to the use of ships and plantation boats. Why choose such a powerful figure in the community with strong business links to England to harass? Alternatively, did they suspect that Laurens had always been involved in illegal trade aboard his plantation boats and had the regulators simply chosen one instance as a convenient excuse to exercise their bureaucratic powers? If this were the case, we would be unlikely to read about it in his personal correspondence and could only speculate about what happened.

What role did his boatmen play in this drama? Why did he want his plantation boat, the *Baker,* to be converted into a speedier sloop model that would require a smaller and lighter crew? Would this have enabled it to outrun customs officials and to slip quietly and quickly in and out of sheltered bays, or was it simply an effort to achieve greater transportation and labor efficiency in the river trade as befitted an astute businessman? It seems likely that the attitudes of his friends and business partners, including ship owners, shipwrights, and even the governor, might have been influenced by Henry Laurens's negative experiences with customs officials and his diminishing loyalty to the Crown. In a larger historical context, did these events associated with boating regulation and a transportation system upon which the colonists were so vitally dependent ultimately contribute to the pro-revolutionary attitudes of many South Carolinians?

As colonists struggled to gain economic and shipping independence, events began to influence trends in boatbuilding. Rice now became a staple crop, and a specialized slave-driven economy developed. Carolina shipwrights designed boats and ships hulls with a specific use in mind: cargo capacity appropriate for rice barrels, a draft to suit the depth of the waterways utilized; and docking needs that suited a particular country factor or planter. Rig design, on the other hand, was chosen to facilitate function or even fashion. Often rigs were modified or changed to suit new needs of trade and warfare.

Vernacular boats like barges and log hull boats, so useful in the estuaries and rivers of the colony, persisted in the design form of personal and naval craft. The Navy Board of South Carolina ordered Mr. McCulley Righton, the Public Boat Keeper, to "immediately Collect together all the Boats, Flatts, and Peteaugus &c Belonging to this State, to purchase a sufficient number of oars and to have in constant readiness."[60] In 1779 the Continental Congress authorized the building of several galleys in Georgia and South Carolina. Paul Pritchard's Hobcaw Creek shipyard in Charleston was authorized to build one of these galleys. Edward Blake, First Commissioner, requested that Pritchards' yard obtain a "large Flatt [barge or flat-bottomed vessel used locally] and have her altered, Sufficiently Strengethened, and Completely fitted as a Galley to mount one Twenty six pound Cannon in the bows and Two smaller guns in the waist to fight them all on either side Occasionally, with stocks to Mount Eight or ten Swevel Guns, and to row with as many oars as possible to be fitted with mast and yards, and to carry two Latteen Sails."[61]

These shallow-draft vessels, powered by both oars and sails, were ideal for the inland waters and played a role in the American Revolution similar to that of the scout boats patrolling the coastline in the early part of the century. This time, oarsmen were slaves from Loyalists' forfeited estates. During this war, the royal governor was so impressed with the utility of these boats that he ordered some to be built "as nearly as possible of the same dimension and construction and force of those of the Enemy" for the British troops. Similarly, these boats were manned by a multicultural boat crews.[62]

By the turn of the nineteenth century, Charleston had became a training center for much of the South Atlantic region. Experienced city artisans taught their slaves a variety of trades, while other slaves were apprenticed to master craftsmen or apprenticed to tradesmen under the provisions of their deceased owners' wills. Free slave children who got into trouble with the law were assigned to the trades as part of a rehabilitative process. Working in the urban areas gave slaves the best opportunities to learn trades, and many owners sent their slaves from other states to workshops in Charleston for instruction in the handicrafts. By the mid-1800s other states were also purchasing and offering high prices for South Carolina slaves "drawn from the rice culture" and with "manufacturing employment" to such an extent that locals were concerned about the "drain" of slaves to the out of the state.[63]

Patroons and boatmen were a critical part of what could be considered an internal slave economy. Over time, earnings from work as artisans in boating and shipping helped slaves to purchase goods and services for themselves and their families. Marketing goods and visiting other plantations presented opportunities to make new social connections, maintain ties with family members dispersed to other plantations or urban settings, and, most significant, to establish new social and economic identities beyond that of a subservient field hand.[64] The Reverend Charles Colcock Jones's sermon to his congregation emphasized the prevalent view of Southern dependency on urban skilled servitude. His question was: "What is their [slaves'] value as an integral part of our population, to ourselves, our country, and our world itself?" He answered his own query, listing "our boatmen on the waters; our mechanics and artisans to build our homes, to work in many trades; our agriculturalists. . . ."[65]

There is more to add to the narrative of the boatman or shipbuilder than a portrayal of scheming maritime operators within an internal slave economy or a reliable source of cheap, semiskilled labor that Southerners could not afford to sacrifice. Complex and ambiguous relationships evolved between the planter and the patroon, the African and the European craftsmen and sailors, fishermen and boatmen. These precarious social dynamics engaged Charleston merchants, South Carolina Assemblymen, and the English merchants in confrontations and tensions in the lead-up to the Revolution and during its aftermath. Legislative acts, plantation logbooks, mechanic petitions, Admiralty records, and merchant correspondence highlight nuances of ambitions, fears, and aggravations with regard to the slaves who dominated numerically and were fast becoming an integral part of a new world. The archaeological record—especially the remains of vernacular boats—are both iconic artifacts and voices for lowcountry slaves and their immersion and long-lasting contribution to a creole society.

Trade and Plantation Sailboats: The Archaeological Record

Five vessels excavated and studied in the coastal regions of South Carolina and Georgia are likely to be plantation or Caribbean trade watercraft. These shipwrecks were named the Mepkin Abbey boat, the Brown's Ferry vessel, the Clydesdale Plantation sloop, the Malcolm boat, and the B&B boat, after either a location or the person who discovered or reported the wreck to state officials. Each has a unique site number associated with a location on a map and a file of archaeological and historical information stored at the South Carolina Institute of Archaeology and Anthropology at the University of South Carolina. These files include map coordinates, excavation dates, determined or believed dates of usage, hull dimensions, scantlings, construction methods, materials, propulsion, purpose, and areas of use. Some projects were part of theses written by students in specialized maritime archaeology programs at Texas A&M or at East Carolina University; others were state research or management projects.

The Malcolm boat was excavated in the Ashley River outside Charleston in 1992. All of the artifacts from the vessel date to the last quarter of the 1700s or the first quarter of the eighteenth century. The boat appears to have had a lengthy usage prior to being stripped and abandoned on the bank of the river. It was constructed of local woods. The pine keelson was of substantial size and was notched over and fastened to each frame. Two rectangular mast steps were carved into the keelson; one was located above the midship frame (approximately one-third of the vessel's length and aft of the stem) and the other step, which was partially plugged, was set further aft, in the forward half of the ship. Maritime archaeologists assess the boat as being designed for strength, with the ability to carry heavy loads. The transom stern was a construction feature that enhanced the vessel's cargo-carrying capacity and seaworthiness for offshore voyages. The boat would have been suited to both offshore and river usage. An artistic reconstruction drawing by former naval architect, William Judd, depicts a functional and aesthetically pleasing boat design.[66]

In 1976 a shipwreck was recovered at Brown's Ferry on the Black River in Georgetown County, South Carolina. The fully laden vessel was carrying twenty-five tons (25,401.2 kg) of bricks when it sank. It has been dated to the middle of the eighteenth century on the basis of a limited number of recovered artifacts.[67] The vessel did not have a keel. It was fitted with a heavy keel plank and was built in the bottom-based construction tradition in which the bottom of the vessel is the main structural component in the overall design. The remaining timbers were fashioned from local woods. The boat had a small transom stern and two mast steps carved into the keelson. In addition to sail, the ship was propelled by the oars and punting poles. The vessel has been described as

Figure 16. Malcolm boat excavations. Courtesy of SCIAA.

the "short haul truck of her time."[68] It was intended strictly for river or inland water use, and its heavy, flat bottom served to facilitate beaching on the riverbanks to load and unload cargo. This boat design was capable of short journeys in coastal waters and could even have been used to make trips to Charleston, approximately seventy-five miles (120.7 km) away from where the wreck was discovered.

A group of students from the Nautical Archaeology Program at Texas A&M University under the direction of Frederick Hocker excavated the Clydesdale Plantation sloop in the Back River, a secondary channel of Savannah River not far from the city, in 1992. The vessel is not easily dated, as it had been stripped and deliberately buried to stabilize a rice bank (levee), but it was probably buried sometime between 1780 and 1820. The upper stem assembly and much of the port side were missing, but the starboard side was preserved nearly to the deck level amidships. The remains were sufficiently preserved to get an accurate idea of the vessel's construction and use. With an original length of forty-three feet nine inches (13.31 m) and a beam of fifteen feet five inches (4.7 m) it had a heavy keel and a transom stern.

A single mast, set forward of amidships, probably supported a sloop rig. The Clydesdale Plantation sloop was a fast, powerful sailing vessel with relatively little cargo capacity. While the hold was constructed tightly enough to have

Figure 17. Profile of Malcolm boat. Courtesy of SCIAA.

carried rice (tight in this case means waterproof), it is doubtful this was its primary purpose, as the vessel would have been better suited to the work of a pilot vessel, taking passengers between Charleston and Savannah, or even to trade as far away as the West Indies or Bermuda. It would have handled well in deep water with its heavy keel, sharp entrance, noticeable deadrise, and long fine run, yet it was small enough to travel the coastal rivers around Savannah.[69]

The Mepkin Abbey wreck was discovered by a sport diver, Drew Ruddy, and studied as a master's thesis topic by Susan Vezeau under the direction of SCIAA at the University of South Carolina and the Nautical Archaeology Program at Texas A&M University. It was a vessel of approximately twenty-three tons (23,369.1 kg) capable of carrying ninety-five barrels of rice, as each ton would hold approximately four barrels. It was very similar to the capacity of the Malcolm boat, which William Judd, a naval draftsman, determined to be between twenty-two and twenty-four tons (22,353–24,385.1 kg). Judd calculated that the Malcolm boat could hold eighty-one barrels. This vessel cannot be dated with any degree of certainty on the basis of its materials, construction methods, and fasteners. Dating only the evidence of the remaining fragments of the vessel provides a range of approximately 150 years, to somewhere in the eighteenth or nineteenth centuries. The recovery and documentation of the stoneware jugs from the wreck narrow the date of this vessel to the second quarter of the nineteenth century. One of the jugs had the maker's mark "SWAINE," associated with pottery manufactured by Thomas and Robert Swaine, who made pottery between 1824 and 1844 in Sutton Heath, England.[70]

A recreational diver, Douglas Boehme, and his teenage daughter Helen discovered and reported the B&B boat. Harry Pecorelli, under the direction of SCIAA, the University of South Carolina, and the Program of Maritime Studies at East Carolina University, studied the vessel. The ship, located in Quinby Creek a tributary of the East Branch of the Cooper River, was fifty-one feet in length and fifteen feet in beam. It consisted of a keel with a keel shoe or plank, eroded stern, disarticulated bow assembly, eroded keelson, outer hull planks, outer hull planks, and no ceiling planking, although ceiling fastenings were present. In contrast to the other boats, this example had a round keel, and there was no notching of the keelson to lock the frames in place (a European shipbuilding technique); some floors were not debarked, and in several places an unfinished tree branch was used as a futtock. Pecorelli surmises that the crudely hewn and unfinished timbers suggest that the boat was built at a plantation, perhaps by slaves, rather in a shipyard by European-trained shipwrights. This illustrates the extent of a Southern plantation sufficiency. While the five boats have some construction features in common, the differences in design and materials used are testimony to builders' ingenuity and to the available resources and labor.[71]

Each boat was fastened with iron nails, iron bolts, and wooden treenails. The woods used in their construction are all found in the lowcountry. Live oak, perfect for compass timbers, was the wood of choice at the end of the eighteenth century at shipyards both in America and in Europe. The B&B boat was made primarily of oak except for the outer hull planks, keel shoe, and treenails. The keels of the Clydesdale sloop and the Malcolm boat and the keel plank of the Brown's Ferry vessel were southern yellow pine. This pine yielded long and straight timbers with enough sap to make it rot-resistant, but it was far softer and less durable than live oak. Three ships had keelsons made from southern yellow pine, while that of the Brown's Ferry vessel was made of cypress. Cypress was also used for treenails on the Mepkin Abbey shipwreck. Cypress likely was used in earlier colonial times for shipbuilding since those trees were plentiful. They grew primarily along the riverbanks and would have been felled to clear fields for rice cultivation, making the wood readily available. This was another factor considered in dating Brown's Ferry vessel. All five vessels were sailing craft.

The Brown's Ferry vessel and perhaps also the Malcolm boat may have carried two masts. The Clydesdale Plantation sloop and the Mepkin Abbey vessel had only single mast steps, but Mepkin Abbey's step was of exceptionally heavy construction and may have been used to modify a vessel that was originally two-masted. Oars and punting poles were found in the Brown's Ferry vessel, and it is likely that these alternate modes of propulsion were used on the other craft as well. There is a six-foot (1.83 m) tide change in the southeastern low-country area every six hours, and all of the intercoastal waters abound with sand bars and oyster beds, making grounding a common occurrence. The Clydesdale Plantation sloop was the only vessel among the five that does not appear to have been specifically designed for hauling cargo, although its hold was made water-tight to carry perishable goods. This suggests that it may have been occasionally used to transport rice or some other grain.

A Final Note

A CANOW missing! A CANOE found! A PETTIAUGER lives on!

Watercraft that traveled the rivers, sounds, and coastline were symbols of a creole heritage with a discernable morphology and social context in multiethnic enterprises, with free and enslaved African playing a central role. These vessels were suited to the new landscape and to the cargoes they were designed to carry, yet were used to achieve traditional European goals of defense, offense, and commerce. Boat usage also allowed enslaved boatmen to undermine the control that wealthy European society wished to have over its bonded property.

Diverse groups of immigrants who worked together with a combination of tension and tenacity created a local boat culture and contributed their efforts as an essential labor force toward building a maritime industry that today colors the character of the legacy still evident in the small coastal communities. This legacy was distinctive to the lowcountry's social, economic, and environmental needs. The immigrants' ideas were not always shared in a formal setting over the drawing board in the master shipwright's quarters but were offered in casual working locations where the immigrants observed a variety hull shapes and rigging designs influenced by their experiences in Carolina, the Caribbean, and their former European or African home environments. In the same way that Charleston's early culturally mixed community of artisans and mechanics represented a boatbuilding traditions that grew out of an amalgamation of various cultures, the city's various groups also needed one another for cooperative boat use ventures that ensured the survival of the colony. At no other time in American history did Africans, Native Americans, and Europeans play such a combined role in an economy that was so intricately tied to rivers and the coastline. They were not a homogenous cultural, ethnic, or occupational group. Sometimes they worked well together; on other occasions they did not. This was not a world that they created together in harmony. It was shaped by the ambitions of the planters, country factors, merchants, and shipwrights who either struggled against or used to their own commercial advantage the efforts of Native American and African slaves from a variety of ethnic groups and Scottish and Irish shipwrights who constantly tried to carve a more autonomous niche for themselves. The lower social classes, such as the deerskin traders, shipyard laborers, plantation boat patroons, and scout and patrol boat captains of European origin, were usually the middlemen caught in the crosscurrents of these interactions. Laboring classes that included Europeans, Africans, and Native Americans may have formed alliances in the earlier colonial period, but these relationships appear to have deteriorated as commerce moved into an urban setting. The frustrations faced by the working-class Europeans who acted as middlemen, competing in the labor market with slaves, were among the paving stones that led to later racial tensions. In summary, boats were an important centerpiece in this dynamic set of relationships. This study attempts to contribute another small piece of identity to the potpourri of immigrants, both bonded and unbonded, who stepped onto Carolina's shores from sailing ships and boarded boats together. Their influence on local boating was probably strongest in the early years of settlement, when the first inhabitants needed all the help they could find in the process of developing a fleet of inland and coastal craft. The riverboat, or periagua, was a distinctive product of this era. The canoe-style hull was the Model-T Ford of Charleston boat culture.

As a final note, research has revealed that in the absence of formal port registration records such as those for colonial ships in the transatlantic trade, probably the most important and prolific source of historic documentation for vernacular craft are the local newspapers. South Carolina's eighteenth-century newspapers regularly ran advertisements for the recovery, discovery, or sale of cypress dugouts, some of which may have conducted coastal and inland journeys. The aquatic utility vehicles of their day, these sailing or rowing single-log dugouts and split-log dugouts carried people and cargoes up and down the rivers of South Carolina's lowcountry and were valued highly by their owners.[1]

In the earliest edition of Charleston's *South Carolina Gazette* on record, in 1732, Edward Scull sought his lost boat: "Gone a Drift or taken from *Col. Brewton's* Bridge, a Cyprus Canoo, call'd the *Old Dolphin,* 26 Foot long, 3 Foot 6 Inches over . . . 40 s Reward." It appears that bridges were a common place to lose a canoe. Thomas Smith advertised in the next week's edition: "Gone Adrift from *Thomas Elliot's* new Bridge . . . a Cyprus Canoe, 22 Foot long, lately topped . . . carries 4 Oars . . . Five Pounds Reward." The list goes on. In another ad, from 1745, the paper describes another missing boat: "lost . . . from *Capt. Frankland's* wharf new canow 3 feet wide, 18 or 19 feet long, single gunnel with 4 oars." Frankland's wharf might have been an unlucky place to keep a canoe. Peter Bonneau ran a similar ad two years later, in 1747, for a "large Cypress Canow 4 feet wide 27 feet long" lost from the same wharf at night, offering a reward of four pounds. One of the most detailed advertisements ran two years later:

> Stolen from my landing on Ashley River, in February last, a large cyprus canow near 30 feet long and about 4 and a half wide, a broad stern; she has 3 or 4 links of chain in a staple drove in her head to fasten rope to; she is supposed to be in some creek near Charles-Town, the rogues who stole her carried 3 barrels of rice with her . . . 5 l.[pound] reward.
>
> *William Cattel*

This ad ran for three weeks. Most ads ran for two or three weeks, seldom longer. Whether this reflects a successful outcome of placing such advertisements is uncertain. The presence of three barrels of rice attests to the small-scale trade most farmers carried out alongside the larger plantations. A similar ad from 1732 describing the disappearance of a "Pettiauger that carries about 30 Barrels of Rice" fetched the same five-pound reward, suggesting that canoes were highly prized by their owners. Jacob Motte suffered a similar fate in 1760 with his sixteen-foot-long canoe, "Taken or went adrift from the bluff at Mout Pleasant, near *Gray's* ferry" and marked on the "head and stem IM," for which he offered an unspecified reward. Also in 1760, William Lawrence ran this ad in the *Gazette:* "Stolen from my landing . . . A CYPRESS CANOW That rows with 4 oars, about 20 feet long and 30 [3] feet wide, and has a new stern seat not finished, and is branded on the forecastle in several places M. Reward of TWO DOLLARS."

Just as often as cypress canoes disappeared, in what constituted the auto theft of its day, and unlike the outcome of most car thefts, canoes were found by other boatmen. As per the laws of the day regarding salvage and finds, it was common for ads to appear announcing where some of those "lost" canoes could be found. John Stuart advertised "a large Cyprus Canoe, about 5 Feet wide and 28 long." It was customary for owners to present some form of proof of ownership, usually by giving a description, and then, after paying for the cost of the ad and providing some reward, to receive their vessel: "giving her true Marks (of which there are several) may have her paying reasonable Charges," ran a notice in the *Gazette* in 1738. In 1743 James Pratt ran a similar ad for a "Cypress Canoe 15 Feet 8 inches long, and 2 Feet 8 inches over, the inside painted red"; the ad ended with reference to payment of proper charges. This ad ran again the following week and a third time with the canoe's latest location, suggesting that the cost of advertising the find was worth the potential payment of "proper charges."

Similar ads offer insight into the dimensions and construction features of cypress dugout canoes. An ad run in the Gazette in 1745 by William Fond'm refers to a "Cypress Canoe" three feet wide and seventeen feet long with a locker in the stern. Another ad, from 1747, merely refers to a "small canow, branded CC in Stern"; owners were to apply to Elizabeth Hill, evidence that women too profited from the salvage of small cypress vessels. A 1748 ad in the *Gazette* reads: "Taken up adrift near Sullivan Island, a Cypres Canow, 4 feet 2 inches wide, 29 feet 6 inches long, and another split Head and Stern with plank in the bottom [expanded split-log] 2 feet 6 inches wide, 15 feet long." Another expanded split-log was mentioned in an ad run in 1749 by John Fryer that refers to a "cypress canow that had been split and widened, near 18 feet long, 3 feet 5 inches wide." Such ads demonstrate that not all expanded split-log boats were of larger dimensions than single-log dugouts. Another ad from 1748 concerns a canoe of similar dimensions: "a Cypress Canow, 3 feet wide, 20 feet long, rows with 4 oars and has a sculling place in her stern"; this ad indicates that not all log boats were equipped with rudders. A ad run in the Gazette in 1758 reveals detailed construction features, no doubt in hopes of turning up the owner: "A Cypress Canow, 3 feet 4 inches wide, 20 feet long, much broken at her head, live oak stem, with a chain 8 feet 4 inches long, has 6 timbers on one side 4 on the other, with 2 oars, also stern seats on each side, 3 rowing seats, 1 fore seat, and 4 row locks, but no head seat, and steers with a rudder . . . the owner may have her again, proving his property, paying the charges and applying to *John Godfrey at Wappo*." Here the actual floors are described as being in a nonsymmetrical arrangement: seats for three rowers, locks for tow, and a rudder for steering. An ad run the following year lists "a cypress canow, about 24 feet long and 4 feet broad, with long stern sheets," demonstrating the use of sail for propulsion, as yet unmentioned.

The consistent run of ads for lost and found canoes suggests that such vessels, though easy to dismiss as crude, ungainly, and insignificant, were rather the contrary. The author encountered a few ads like this one, run in the *Gazette* in 1774: "WANTED, A CANOE, Thirty Feet long, and Four Feet Ten Inches wide." Such specificity attests to both the popular use of canoes along the waterways of the lowcountry and the availability of buyers who were knowledgeable about their dimensions. Rarely did ads actually list a canoe for sale, like this one, run in the *Port Royal Gazette* in 1781: "A Commodious CANOE, 26 feet long, and upwards of five feet wide, rows with six oars, sails," which affirms the use of sail on small vernacular craft. A similar ad from was placed by Nicholl Turnbull: "VERY HANDSOME Cypress Six oared CANOE."

As mentioned, cypress was used in the construction of larger vessels. A packet boat, *Two Brothers,* was listed in the *Savannah Advertiser* in 1803 at "36 feet keel, 39 feet long, 6 feet 3 inches . . . . Is built of cypress and cedar." The Brown's Ferry Wreck was composed of pine and cypress, and the Mepkin Abbey wreck utilized cypress, as well, showing the utilization of the wood by southeastern shipwrights in vessels larger than plantation boats. Despite being softwood, cypress is known for its resistance to rot and damp, which made it a desirable choice. One ambitious Charlestonian whose name appears in land deals and other advertisements placed an ad in the *Gazette* in 1751 describing "a cypress canow about 17 feet long, 3 feet wide. Any person owning the same, may have her, on paying 40lb., which he paid for taking up the same." Obviously the market for cypress canoes was strong. The *Accommodation,* its age unknown at the time of sale, managed to fetch its seller $150 in 1855.

While the remaining material culture representing the rich and varied story of enslaved watermen and the watercraft they crewed still resides quietly in rivers, marshess and museums, another form of this maritime heritage survives more vibrantly in the form of a experimental project in North Carolina that is constructing a historic periagua. The project was a unique partnership of the Perquimans County Restoration Association and the North Carolina Maritime Museum. In November 2003, hull construction began in Beaufort at the North Carolina Maritime Museum's Watercraft Center with boatbuilder Craig Wright overseeing the construction of the periagua and utilizing a combination of historical records and his understanding of materials and construction techniques of the day. The builder designed a vessel based on historical records that would be approximately thirty feet long with two masts reaching the height of twenty-five feet and with with rowing stations for at least six oars (sweeps)—basically a hollowed-out cypress tree log, split in half with a plank keel added between the two halves. The plan was not only to build the vessel but also to experience sailing and rowing it. After the builders completed the interior fitting, rowing trials began for this unique historic vessel. There are eight rowing stations, each equipped with a twelve-foot-long sweep. The vision is that the Periauger Project will be an important tool for regional tourism development as it visits port towns in the region and provides a dynamic living maritime history experience.[2]

Notes

Preface

1. "Periagua" is spelled many different ways in the South Carolina colonial records (e.g., piragua, periogo, pettyager, petiager). The Spanish (*piragua*), Portuguese (*piroga*), and French (*pirogue*) terms all translate to "dugout canoe." Apart from South Carolina, periaguas as a working boat type were also used in other eastern states during the colonial era. For example, Cornelius Vanderbilt, who built large shipping and rail enterprises into cornerstones of the American economy, frequently "deployed his old periauger as a lorry delivering rum beer and other desirables for sale to the crews of newly arriving packet ships in New York Harbor." As a boy, he purchased a periauger for one hundred dollars—his first boat. Edward Reneham, *Commodore: The Life of Cornelius Vanderbilt* (New York: Basic Books, 2009), 26, 29, 52. Pettiaugers were used by the Continental army in 1776. General Washington told General Israel Putnam, then commanding at New York City, to "Let the Committee [of Safety] by all Means have the Pettiauger to cruize off the Back of the Island [probably Long Island]." http://www.continentalline.org/articles/0001/000101.htm (accessed May 19, 2012).

2. Henry Laurens to Timothy Creamer, Charleston, June 20, 1794, 4: 319; Henry Laurens to John Smith, Charleston, May 30, 1765; Henry Laurens to John Smith, Charleston, October 1, 1765, 5: 11, all in George C. Rogers Jr. et al. (eds.), *The Papers of Henry Laurens* (Columbia: University of South Carolina Press, 1972–2001).

3. John Fauchereaud Grimke (ed.), *The Public Laws of South Carolina from Its First Establishment as British Province Down to the Year 1790* (Philadelphia: R. Aitken and Son, 1790), 2. See "An Act to prevent the Stealing and Taking Away of Boats and Canoes, March 16, 1695–1696, No. 126," in Thomas Cooper and David James McCord (eds.), *The Statutes at Large of South Carolina* (Columbia, S.C.: A. S. Johnston, 1836–1841), 2: 105, 7: 409, 426–42. In 1747 another act declared that the theft of a pettiguar or schooner would be considered a felony punishable by death. In addition, the culprit would be excluded and barred from the benefit of clergy. Variations of this harsh legislation were repeated numerous times throughout the eighteenth century, revealing that there was considerable fear that slaves who were involved managing these boats were likely to use them for travel and escape.

4. "The Petition of Merchants, Traders, Planters, and Other Interested in the Trade and Prosperity of South Carolina and Georgia," December 21, 1756. Rogers et al., *Laurens Papers*, 2: 379.

5. Jeffrey Bolster, *Black Jacks: African American Men in the Age of Sail* (Cambridge, Mass.: Harvard University Press, 1998); James Barker Farr, *Black Odyssey: The Seafaring Traditions of African Americans* (New York: Peter Lang, 1991); Marcus Rediker, *Between the Devil and the Deep Blue Sea: Merchant Seamen, Pirates and the Anglo-American World: 1700–1750* (New York: Cambridge University Press, 1987); Grace Turner, "Bahamian Ship Grafitti," *International Journal of Nautical Archaeology* 35:2 (2006): 253–73; Peter Wood, *Black Majority: Negroes in South Carolina from 1670 through the Stono Rebellion.* (New York: W. W. Norton, 1974); Charles Joyner, *Down by the Riverside: A South Carolina Slave Community* (Urbana: University of Illinois Press, 1984); David Cecelski, *The Waterman's Song: Slavery and Freedom in Maritime North Carolina* (Chapel Hill: University of North Carolina Press, 2001); Kevin Dawson, "Enslaved Swimmers and Divers in the Atlantic World," *Journal of American History* 92:4 (March 2006): 1327–55.

6. Leland Ferguson, *Uncommon Ground: Archaeology and Early African America, 1650–1800* (Washington, D.C.: Smithsonian Institution Press, 1992).

7. Mulattoes were first-generation persons of white and black ancestry. Mustees were first-generation persons of Native American and black ancestry.

8. These general history texts provide a background to South Carolina's trading activities and early settlers: Robert M. Weir, *Colonial South Carolina* (Millwood, N.Y.: KTO Press, 1983); Walter Edgar, *South Carolina: A History* (Columbia: University of South Carolina, 1998). More specific immigrant settlement studies include Amy E. Friedlander, "Carolina Huguenots: A Study in Colonial Pluralism," Ph.D. diss., Emory University, 1979; Henry Augustus Middleton Smith, "The Orange Quarter and the First French Settlers in South Carolina," *South Carolina Historical and Genealogical Magazine* 18 (1917): 101–23; John P. Thomas, "The Barbadians in Early South Carolina," *South Carolina Historical and Genealogical Magazine* 2 (April 1930): 75–92; David Dobson, *Directory of Scots in the Carolinas, 1680–1830* (Baltimore: Genealogical Publishing Company, 1986); Joseph Williams, *Whence the Black Irish of Jamaica* (New York: Dial Press, 1932). Williams's work relies on the Calender of State Papers 1661–1668, no. 528, Colonial Services, America and West Indies; Jack P. Greene, "Colonial South Carolina and the Caribbean Connection," *South Carolina Historical Magazine* 88 (1987): 192–210. The *South Carolina Gazette* is also filled with advertisements for cargoes and lists of ports of call for colonial shipping.

9. *South Carolina Gazette*, July 9–16, 1763.

10. Patricia Causey Nichols, *Voices of Our Ancestors: Language Contact in Early South Carolina* (Columbia: University of South Carolina Press, 2009).

11. Charles Joyner, *Shared Traditions: Southern History and Folk Culture* (Urbana: University of Illinois Press, 1999), 150.

12. Timothy Hall Breen, "Creative Adaptations: Peoples and Cultures," in Jack P. Greene and Jack R. Pole (eds.), *Colonial British America: Essays in the New History of the Modern Era* (Baltimore, Md.: Johns Hopkins University Press, 1984), 197.

Chapter 1. The Colonial Cultural Landscape

1. Alexander Samuel Salley (ed.), *Narratives of Early Carolina: 1650–1708* (New York: Barnes and Noble, 1967), 108.

2. Roy Merrens (ed.), *The Colonial South Carolina Scene* (Columbia: University of South Carolina Press, 1977), 87, 92.

3. Lincoln Stoller, "The Indian's Apprentice," *The Wooden Boat* 74 (January/February 1987): 27–33. The Indians of Central America, especially in the coastal regions of Honduras, Nicaragua, Guatamala, and Panama, may be directly related to the southeastern tribes as well as to the Arawak and Carib, who were more direct ancestors. Carribean trade winds blow directly east to west. Anthropologists hypothesize that not only Carib and Arawak survivors but also some remnants of the Creek and Seminole moved west.

4. Charles Hudson (ed.), *The Juan Pardo Expeditions: Explorations of the Carolinas and Tennessee 1566–1568* (Washington, D.C.: Smithsonian Institution Press, 1984), 132–36. This volume is an account of the contact situations between the Spanish and the Indians in the southeastern United States. One of the means Hudson uses to place the Pardo route in modern geographic space is through the use of archaeology. He provides the reader with translated journals in an appendix and is careful to give possible alternative explanations for the identification and locations of sites.

5. Paul Hulton (ed.), *The Work of Jacques le Moyne, a Huguenot Artist in France, Florida, and England* (London: British Museum Publications, 1977); Paul Hulton (ed.), *America 1585: The Complete Drawings of John White* (Chapel Hill: University of North Carolina Press, 1984).

6. Hulton, *John White,* 118. John White was the official artist for the 1585 voyage to the Carolinas. It has been suggested that he was stylistically influenced by the French artist Jacques le Moyne, although there are many more canoes in John White's works. See Plates 8, 9, 10, 11, 12, 14, 15, 16, and 17. This publication reproduces seventy-six watercolors from his collection that represent the best pictorial record of North American Native Americans. The originals are now housed in the British Museum. Paul Hulton, the editor, was deputy keeper in the Department of Prints and Drawings of the British Museum.

7. William Bartram, *Travels and Other Writings: Travels through North and South Carolina, Georgia East and Florida, 1773–1774* (Savannah, Ga.: Beehive Press, 1973), 407.

8. Ibid.,198, 489.

9. Ibid., 402.

10. John Lawson, *A New Voyage to South Carolina* (Chapel Hill: University of North Carolina Press, 1967), 140; Henry S. Burrage (ed.), "The First Voyage made to the Coasts of America, by Captain Arthur Barlowe," *Early English and French Voyages 1534–1608: Original Narratives of Early American History* (New York: C. Scribner, 1906), 5: 127; Kathy Manning, "Water Travel of the Southeastern Indians," paper presented at the Thirty-sixth Annual Meeting of the Southeastern Archaeological Conference, University of Georgia (South Carolina Institute of Archaeology and Anthropology files, 1979).

11. Lawson, *A New Voyage to South Carolina,* 38; Maurice Matthews, "A Contemporary View of South Carolina," *South Carolina Historical Magazine* 50–58 (1949–1959): 153–59.

12. Gene Waddell, *Indians of the South Carolina Lowcountry, 1562–1751* (Spartanburg, S.C.: Reprint Company, 1974), 39. This source is a detailed history of the Native Americans in proximity to Charleston. It summarizes material about specific tribes and place names and includes general accounts of language, foods, and ceremonies. It also provides a comparison with Native Americans who lived in other areas. This author used eyewitness accounts of early travelers as his source.

13. Walter Edgar, *South Carolina: A History* (Columbia: University of South Carolina Press, 1998).

14. Alan Feduccia (ed.), *Catesby's Birds of Colonial America* (Chapel Hill: University of North Carolina Press, 1985), 147, 161.

15. William M. Rivers, *Historical Sketches of South Carolina* (Charleston, S.C.: McCarter and Company, 1856), 115. The appendix contains many useful examples of correspondence from the Lord Proprietors and highlights the tensions in the relationship between the Lords and the governors. Most problems revolved around what constituted the governors' perceived duties and powers in the colony. There is also advice about relationships with the Native Americans and others, including the "Scotch and Divers others considerable persons who have intentions to become settlers in Carolina" (p. 398).

16. Fedduccia, *Birds,* 147, 161.

17. Alexander S. Salley (ed.), *Records in the British Public Office Relating to South Carolina* (Columbia: Historical Commission of South Carolina, 1946), 4: 84.

18. Ibid., 4: 88.

19. Thomas Hatley, *The Dividing Paths: Cherokees and South Carolinians through the Era of the Revolution* (London: Oxford University Press, 1993), 161. European concepts of profit, credit, and debt were gradually incorporated into Cherokee ideology about commerce. Traditionally, accumulation of wealth was overridden by the concept of gift-giving. In other words, debt did not always have the same meaning to Native Americans that it had for the colonists. To the Native Americans, gift-giving was not considered a burden but a moving gift creating a link between the creditor and the debtor. Trading items went through periods of greater and lesser popularity with Native Americans. Once the market for a particular type of good was satisfied, demand decreased, even for guns. This perplexed traders, who realized that they could make a bigger profit on scissors, earrings, and other trifles than on guns and ammunition. Attitudes also changed about the concept of trade with Europeans. The Native American boating traders who negotiated on behalf of the European were the middlemen in these transactions, equipped with greater insights into the local needs.

20. Verner Crane, *Southern Frontier, 1670–1732* (New York: W. W. Norton, 1981), 254; Hatley, *Dividing Paths,* 33, 45. Goods desired by Native Americans did not always represent some form of technological advantage. The Cherokee did not necessarily want guns for more efficient hunting; they wanted them for the noise and smoke they created, which was incorporated into new ritualistic greetings or other signs of good will. In 1756 at Fort Prince George, Captain Raymond Demere wrote, "The Indians are now about me, and will not disperse . . . they have earnestly requested of me that the great guns might be fired again for [one of their messenger's] good and safe return." Other goods were transformed

from European uses to their own cultural context. For example, mirrors, Delftware, and faience shards were recycled as expressions of status in the form of jewelry or burial goods. Europeans knew what items were popular trade goods but were not always clear on how particular items were specifically relevant to the Native American culture.

21. Elmer D. Johnson and Kathleen Lewis Sloan, *South Carolina: A Documentary Profile of the Palmetto State* (Columbia: University of South Carolina Press, 1971), 4–5.

22. Theodore H. Lewis, "The Narrative of the Expedition of Hernando De Soto by the Gentleman of Elvas," in *Spanish Explorers of the United States: Original Narratives of Early American History, 1528–1543* (New York: Scribner's,1907), 203.

23. John R. Swanton, "Indians of the South Eastern United States," *Bureau of American Ethnology Bulletin* 27 (1946), 596; Hudson, *Pardo Expeditions,* 314.

24. Lee Newsome and Barbara A. Purdy, "Florida Canoes: A Maritime Heritage from the Past," *The Florida Anthropologist* 43:3 (September 1990).These archaeologists view the development of technology to produce and use canoes as an analyzable part of the social infrastructure of both prehistoric and historic Indians. Behavior patterns associated with procuring the materials and manufacturing and using the canoes involved considerable energies. The ramifications of these patterns are apparent in many realms of Indian culture —including economic and social behaviors and rituals—providing continuities through time and space. The majority of research devoted to the material culture record and history of the Southeastern canoe form and its manufacture has been conducted in Florida. Other sources of information include Wilfred T. Neill, "Dugouts of the Mikasuki Seminole," *The Florida Anthropologist* 6:3 (1953), 77–84; Wilfred T. Neill,"Coracles or Skinboats of the Southeastern Indians," *The Florida Anthropologist* 7:4 (1954): 119–26; Lynn Harris, "Sea and Swampcraft: The Utility of Canoe and Canoe Built Vessels in the Lowcountry," *Legacy: The Newsletter of the South Carolina Institute of Archaeology and Anthropology, University of South Carolina* 2:3 (December 1977): 20–22.

25. Waddell, *Indians,* 4, 363 fn. 16. Upon arrival in South Carolina, waves of white immigrants encountered multiple waterway Native American societies that were embroiled in disruptive contacts with French and Spanish explorers. The colonists identified nineteen tribal communities after whom they named rivers. The Waccamaw, Sewee, and Winyah lived around Charleston. South of Charleston, along the coast, the Winbee, Combahee, Ashepoo, Edisto, Bohicket, Stono, Kiawah, Etiwan, Wando, and Coosa resided. In 1605 Spanish expedition leaders reported meetings with Kiawah, Etiwan, and Stono Native Americans living on or near Charleston Harbor. By 1682, Kiawah were settled on both sides of the Ashley River.

In 1682 European occupation began along Cooper River and extended toward Goose Creek by 1710. During the early settlement years, Wando lived both along the northern edge of Charleston Harbor and southward where the Wando River entered the Cooper River. By 1699, smallpox had decimated the Wando community. Stono lived near the mouth of North Edisto River in 1663 and along the Stono River in 1682; around 1695 they moved to Seabrook Island. Ibid., 4, 363 fn. 16.

26. Richard Sheridan, *Sugar and Slavery: An Economic History of the British West Indies* (Baltimore, Maryland: Johns Hopkins University Press, 1973), 124–47. This work draws on information from the Public Record Offices in London and in West Indies Islands such

as Jamaica. Private letter books in Antigua and Scotland are also cited. See also Jack P. Greene, "Colonial South Carolina and the Caribbean Connection," *South Carolina Historical Magazine* 88 (1987): 197–198.

27. Richard S. Dunn, *Sugar and Slaves: The Rise of the Planter Class in the English West Indies, 1624–1713* (Chapel Hill: University of North Carolina Press, 1972), 230–31. The Dutch slave trade in the seventeenth century has not yet been systematically researched. Records in the Netherlands may still reveal how many Africans were brought to the colonies and the locations from which they were carried by Dutch ships before enforcement of the English Navigation Acts cut off the supply. The activities of the English Royal African Company, which operated between 1673 and 1688, are much easier to trace.

28. Sheridan, *Sugar and Slavery.*

29. Aubrey Gwynn, "Cromwell's Policy of Transportation," *Irish Quarterly Review* 19:76 (December 1930): 608; Jill Sheppard, *The Redlegs of Barbadoes* (Millwood, N.Y.: KTO Press, 1977), 18. A large amount of Sheppard's information is derived from the Barbados Museum Historical Society journals and from immigrant shipping lists in the city of Bristol, in the United Kingdom. See also Joseph Williams, *Whence the Black Irish of Jamaica* (New York: Dial Press, 1932), 12; his work relies on the Calendar of State Papers 1661–1668, no. 528, Colonial Services, America and West Indies.

30. Edgar, *South Carolina,* 51; Amy E. Friedlander, "Carolina Huguenots: A Study in Colonial Pluralism," Ph.D. diss., Emory University, 1979, 86.

31. Sheppard, *Redlegs,* 12.

32. Agnes Baldwin, *First Settlers of South Carolina* (Columbia: University of South Carolina Press, 1969).

33. Ibid., 3; Maxwell Clayton Orvin, *Historic Berkeley County, 1671–1900* (Charleston, S.C. Comprint, 1973), 2. Amy Friedlander contends that historians have not looked much at ethnicity during the colonial period (vii).

34. Edgar, *South Carolina,* 49.

35. Langdon Cheves (ed.), *Shaftesbury Papers,* Collections of the South Carolina Historical Society, Charleston, 1897, 240–41, 246, 462, 333.

36. William C. Fleetwood, *Tidecraft: The Boats of South Carolina, Georgia and Northeastern Florida, 1550–1950* (Tybee Island, Ga.: W.B.G. Marine Press, 1995), 25; Baldwin, *First Settlers,* 1969.

37. Fleetwood, *Tidecraft,* 87.

38. William A. Baker, *Colonial Vessels: Some Seventeenth Century Designs* (Barre, Mass.: Barre Publishing Company, 1962), describes some common types of ships:

Pink: a small sailing vessel with a sharply narrowed stern and an overhanging transom.

Ketch: a two-masted fore-and-aft-rigged sailing vessel with a mizzenmast stepped aft of a taller mainmast but forward of the rudder.

Galley: a single-decked ship of shallow draft, propelled by sails and oars and used by troop ships with up to sixty rowers in the colonial era.

Brig: a sailing vessel with two square-rigged masts. It is not to be confused with a brigantine, which has different rigging. In the narrow technical field of sailing rigs, a brig is distinct from a three-masted ship by virtue of having only two masts.

Snow or *Snaw:* the largest of all old two-masted vessels with square sails on both masts but a small trysail mast, sometimes called a *snowmast,* stepped immediately abaft the mainmast.

Bark, barque, or barc: a sailing vessel with three or more masts fore-and-aft sails, on the aftermost mast and square sails on all other masts.

Dogger: a development of the ketch, square-rigged on the main mast and carrying a lugsail on the mizzen, with two jibs on a long bowsprit. The boats were generally short, wide-beamed, and small.

Shallop: a light boat used for rowing in shallow water or a small open boat fitted with oars or sails, or both, and used primarily in shallow waters.

Sloop: a single-masted, fore-and-aft-rigged sailing boat with a short standing bowsprit or none at all and a single headsail set from the forestay.

Shallop: a light boat used for rowing in shallow water or a small open boat fitted with oars or sails or both and used primarily in shallow waters.

Lighter: a barge used to move goods in a port or to load and unload ships not secured to a pier.

Moses boat: a square-sterned rowing boat with a rocker keel and a high sheer used as a lighter to handle casks.

Dory: a flat-bottomed skiff that evolved from a planked canoe.

Flatboat: a rectangular flat-bottomed boat with square ends used to transport passengers, goods, and livestock along rivers and on inland waters.

Wherrie or wherry: a rowing boat used for carrying passengers in rivers or canals, rowed by either two men with long oars or a single man with short oars or sculls.

39. Michael B. Alford, "Origins of the Carolina Split Dugout Canoes," *The International Journal of Nautical Archaeology* 21:3 (1992), 191–203; John Lawson, *A New Voyage to Carolina* (Chapel Hill: University of North Carolina Press, 1967).

40. Michael B. Alford, "French Sources of Vernacular Boat Building Practices in the Carolinas," *Underwater Archaeology Proceedings from the Society for Historical Archaeology Conference,* Kansas City, Missouri, 1993, 47.

41. Fleetwood, *Tidecraft,* 2; John Cummins, *The Voyage of Christopher Columbus* (New York: St. Martin's Press, 1992).

42. Cummins, *Voyage,* 524.

43. Robin Law, "Trade and Politics behind the Slave Coast: The Lagoon Traffic and the Rise of Lagos, 1500–1800," *Journal of African History* 24 (1983): 321–23, 333. Law's sources include the recollections of Ochifekouede, an Ijebu from the lagoon-side town of Makun who operated as a lagoon trader and traveled extensively. Observations by Portuguese and Dutch traders provide insights into the variety of uses for canoes and the distances traveled.

44. Ibid., 325; Augusto Epifanio Da Silva (ed.), *Esmeraldo de Situ Orbis* (Lisbon: Sociedade de Geografia de Lisboa,1975), 117.

45. Philip Curtin, *The Atlantic Slave Trade: A Census* (Madison: University of Wisconsin, 1969); Peter Wood, *Black Majority: Negroes in South Carolina from 1670 through the Stono Rebellion* (New York: Knopf, 1974); Daniel Littlefield, *Rice and Slaves: Ethnicity and*

the Slave Trade in South Carolina (Baton Rouge: Louisiana State University Press, 1981); Dunn, *Sugar and Slaves.*

46. Antonio Salas et al., "Charting the Ancestry of African Americans," *American Journal of Human Genetics* 77:4 (October 2005): 676–80; Antonio Salas et al., "The African Diaspora: Mitochondrial DNA and the Atlantic Slave Trade," *American Journal of Human Genetics* 74:3 (March 2004): 454–465. Curtin, *The Atlantic Slave Trade.*

47. Carl Bridenbaugh and Roberta Bridenbaugh, *No Peace beyond the Line: The English in the Caribbean 1624–1690* (New York: Oxford University Press, 1972), 240.

48. George C. Rogers Jr. et al. (eds.), *The Papers of Henry Laurens* (Columbia: University of South Carolina Press, 1972–2001), 2: 348.

49. Charles Boxer, *Four Centuries of Portuguese Expansion* (Berkeley: University of California Press, 1963), 56; Weir, *Colonial South Carolina*, 192–193; Michael Mullin, *Africa in America: Slave Acculturation and Resistance in the American South* (Urbana: University of Illinois Press, 1992), 187, 282. This author states that the "Gullah" people of South Carolina are most likely descended from Angolans. In 1730 an Anglican missionary from St. Paul's parish in the heart of the sea islands described the Gullah as very isolated and being like a "Nation within a Nation. . . . In all country settlements, they live in contiguous houses, . . . they labor together and converse almost wholly amongst themselves." The cultural isolation of the Gullah may have preserved certain skills and social traditions that can be traced to Congolese-Angolan peoples. Scholars from Lorenzo Turner to Joseph Holloway, Margaret Creel, and Robert F. Thompson are divided over which African region should be assigned precedence in connection with the origins and development of the Lowcountry's "peculiar people," the Gullah. For more detailed discussion refer to Lorenzo Turner, *Africanisms in the Gullah Dialect* (New York, 1944); Margaret Washington Creel, *A Peculiar People: Slave Religion and Community Culture Among the Gullahs* (New York: New York University Press, 1988).

50. Greene, "Colonial South Carolina and the Caribbean Connection." In the late 1600s, the colony could be described as specializing in lumber production and animal farming, particularly cattle. For at least one generation, the early colony functioned as intended, that is, as an adjunct to the Barbadian economy. It developed a vigorous grazing economy that rivaled that of Jamaica. In return for Jamaican sugar products and African slaves, South Carolina sent beef, pork, corn, lumber, naval stores, and Indian slaves to Barbados, the Leeward Islands, and Jamaica. Soon South Carolina's economy ceased to depend on trade with the Caribbean islands. In addition, provisioning privateers and pirates and especially trading large quantities of goods with the Native Americans contributed to the early wealth of the colony

51. Converse Clowse, *Economic Beginnings in Colonial South Carolina, 1670–1730* (Columbia: University of South Carolina Press, 1971), 90, 91, 181.

52. Salley, *British Records,* 4: 81.

53. Nicholas Olsberg, "Ship Registers in the South Carolina Archives, 1734–1780," *South Carolina and Historical and Genealogical Magazine* 74 (October 1973): 189–299.

54. Ibid.

55. The insistence that coastal trade vessels enter and clear customs imposed considerable expense on ship owners. The 1766 Revenue Act was intended designed to prevent

the smuggling of foreign molasses into New England, but it put an unreasonable burden on the coastal trade in southern colonies like South Carolina and Georgia. Most customs officials did not enforce these provisions, realizing the cost and inconvenience to planters, despite the Act. Customs collector Daniel Moore was an exception; in the case of Henry Laurens in 1767 he argued that the ship *Active* was carrying enumerated goods without bonds or certificates.

56. Charles M. Andrews, *The Colonial Period of American History: England's Commercial and Colonial Policy* (New Haven: Yale University Press, 1938), 171–73; Weir, *Colonial South Carolina*, 161.

57. "In order to ascertain the true burthen of a ship, we ought to find the place of the light-water line, and thence calculate the number of cubic feet below the line of floatation: as the product, deduct from the number of cubic feet contained at the load-draught, would show the real capacity by which the tonnage may be computed: and, if the difference be multiplied by the weight of a cubic foot of sea water, 64 3/8 lbs., the product, divided by 2240 (the number of lbs. in a ton), will give the true burthen in tons." Records of Wills, Inventories, and Miscellaneous Records for Charleston County, South Carolina, 1671–1868, Charleston County Public Library, South Carolina History Collections. Tonnage is a measure of the size or cargo-carrying capacity of a ship. The term derives from the taxation paid on *tuns* or casks of wine and was later used in reference to the weight of a ship's cargo; however, in modern maritime usage, "tonnage" specifically refers to a calculation of the volume or cargo volume of a ship. It is incorrect to use the term "tonnage" to refer to the loaded or empty weight of the vessel itself. In 1678 Thames shipbuilders used a method that assumed that a ship's burden would be three-fifths of its displacement, since tonnage is calculated by multiplying length x beam x draft x block coefficient, all divided by 35 cubic feet per ton of seawater.

58. Michael J. Jarvis, "Maritime Masters and Seafaring Slaves in Bermuda, 1680–1783," *William and Mary Quarterly* 59 (July 2002): 585–682.

59. Ralph Wilbanks, "A Progress Report on the Small Watercraft Project in South Carolina," *Institute of Archaeology and Anthropology* 12:3–4 (1980): 17–27; Ralph Wilbanks and Katherine Singley Dannenberg, "Small Watercraft Project Update," *South Carolina Institute of Archaeology and Anthropology* 17:1 (1985): 1–5.

60. Harris, "Sea and Swamp Craft"; Lynn Harris, "Public Education and Submerged Smallcraft Documentation in South Carolina, "*Museum Smallcraft Association Transactions* 3 (1997): 46–53; Lynn Harris, "Flowing Timelines: Maritime Heritage Trails in South Carolina." *Sandlapper Magazine* (Summer 1999): 812.

61. Ralph Wilbanks, "The Roots Site a Post-Contact Canoe," unpublished manuscript, South Carolina Institute of Archaeology and Anthropology, University of South Carolina, Columbia.

62. Beta Analytic, "Report of Radio Carbon Dating Analysis," letter dated May 1999, on file at Charleston Field Office, South Carolina Institute of Archaeology and Anthropology.

63. Lee Anne Newsome and Barbara Purdy, "Florida Canoes: A Maritime Heritage from the Past," *Florida Anthropologist* 43:3 (1990): 164–180. Ralph Wilbanks, "A Progress Report on the Small Watercraft Project in South Carolina," *Institute of Archaeology and Anthropology* 12:3–4 (1980): 17–27.

Chapter 2. Traders, Scouts, and Ferrymen

1. Alexander Salley (ed.), *Records in the British Public Office Relating to South Carolina, 1698–1700* (Columbia, S.C.: Crowson-Stone Printing Company, 1947), 4: 189–90.

2. Roy Merrens (ed.), *The Colonial South Carolina Scene* (Columbia: University of South Carolina Press, 1977), 65.

3. Salley, *British Records,* 5: 203.

4. Ibid., 5: 207.

5. William R. Snell, "Indian Slavery in Colonial South Carolina, 1671–1795," Ph.D. diss., University of Alabama, 1972, 51, 77.

6. Ibid., 77.

7. Philip M. Brown, "Early Indian Trade in the Development of South Carolina Politics, Economics, and Social Mobility during the Proprietary Period," *South Carolina Historical Magazine* 76 (1975): 125.

8. Ibid., 121, 126.

9. Gene Waddell, *Indians of the South Carolina Lowcountry* (Spartenburg, S.C.: Reprint Company, 1980), 293.

10. Chapman Milling, *Red Carolinians* (Columbia: University of South Carolina Press, 1969), 208.

11. Warner O. Moore, "The Largest Exporters of Deerskins from Charleston, 1735–1775," *South Carolina Historical Magazine* 76 (1975): 144–45. For the exporter, the economic value and the supply of deerskins varied depending on circumstances such as the existence of international conflicts and Native American wars. Deerskins were one of the most valued commodities in the first three decades of the 1700s and for this reason were considered a valued prize in the colonial tension among England, France, and Spain. After indigo was introduced in the 1740s, deerskins were pushed into second place in the export trade; see Verner Crane, *The Southern Frontier, 1670–1732* (Ann Arbor: University of Michigan Press, 1929. Reissue), 111–12.

12. William C. Fleetwood, *Tidecraft: The Boats of South Carolina, Georgia and Northeastern Florida, 1550–1950* (Tybee Island, Ga.: W.B.G. Marine Press, 1995), 35.

13. Ibid., 38; Kristin Hvidt, *Van Reck's Voyage to Georgia in 1736* (Savannah, Ga.: Beehive Press, 1980), 37.

14. McDowell, *Indian Commissioners,* 172, 194, 217, 243.

15. Ibid., 113, 123, 136.

16. Ibid., 99, 101, 102, 196,197.

17. Larry Ivers, "Scouting the Inland Passage, 1685–1737," *South Carolina Historical Magazine* 73 (July 1972): 117–29.

18. Alexander S. Salley, *Journal of the Commons House of Assembly of South Carolina, 1702* (Columbia, S.C.: The State Company, 1932): 66–67.

19. See Thomas Cooper and David J. McCord, *The Statutes at Large of South Carolina* (Columbia, S.C.: A. S. Johnston, 1836–1841), 2: 10, 11, 24, 610; 7: 32; 9: 623, 624 for acts passed about patrol boats.

20. Salley, *Commons House, 1692–1706*: 79.

21. Joseph Barnwell (ed.), "Fort King George: Journal of Captain John Barnwell," *South Carolina Historical Magazine* 27 (1926): 95,193,194, 200; Virginia Steele Wood and

Mary Bullard (eds.), *Journal of a Visit to the Georgia Islands of St. Catherines, Green, Ossabaw, Sapelo, St. Simons, Jekyll, and Cumberland: With Comments on the Florida Islands of Amelia, Talbot, and St. George, in 1753* (Macon, Ga.: Mercer University Press, 1996), 1–5.

22. Salley, *Commons House, 1692–1706*: 69; Salley, *Commons House, 1727*: 101; Ivers, *Inland Passage,* 117–29; *South Carolina Gazette,* May 12, 1740.

23. The whaleboats, also referred to as surfboats, changed little in the two centuries of deep-sea whaling; the workboats were round hulled and double ended to facilitate movement forward and backward through the surf and were propelled by a combination of oars and sails. See W. S. Tower, *A History of the American Whale Fishers* (Philadelphia: University of Pennsylvania, 1907), 86. The only significant change in these whaleboats was in size, which increased from a length of twenty feet in 1720 to an average of around twenty-eight feet, with some as long as thirty-eight feet well into the early twentieth century. Alexander Starbuck, *History of the American Whale Fishery from Its Earliest Inception to the Year 1876* (New York: Castle, 1989), 123, provides a further description of whaleboats/surf boats and their fittings. These boats were designed to withstand the peril of the chase and the value of the prize. They were designed with these attributes in mind: lightness and form, carrying capacity in relation to weight and seagoing qualities, speed and facility of movement, most advantageous placement of men to take advantage of their own raw power, adaption of the length of the oar and its placement, and simplicity of construction. Thus, the boats had long, sharp, and clean-cut hull lines at the bow and stern, swelling to six feet amidships, and a buoyant, round bottom. The gunwale and keel, twenty-two inches apart, were the heaviest parts, providing stiffness to the whole vessel. The thwarts were supported by knees of a great strength They were either lashed to the side or stowed aboard the larger whale ships.

24. Barnwell, "Journal," 201.

25. Ivers, "Inland Passage," 121–23.

26. Cooper and McCord, *Statutes,* 2: 608.

27. Ibid., 3: 108–9.

28. Salley, *British Records,* 5: 58.

29. Ibid.

30. Ibid., 5: 222–24.

31. *South Carolina Gazette,* September 1–8, 1739.

32. *South Carolina Gazette,* August 18–25, 1739.

33. Weir, *Colonial South Carolina,* 51; George D. Terry, *Champaign Country: A Social History of an Eighteenth Century Lowcountry Parish in South Carolina, St. Johns, Berkeley County* (Columbia: University of South Carolina, 1981), 13.

34. Weir, *Colonial History,* 123–235.

35. Cooper and McCord, *Statutes,* 3: 204, 252, 354. These statutes provide details about the regulations linked to economic activities at the Ashley River and Childesbury landing settlements.

36. Terry, *Social History,* 194; William Barr, "Childesbury and Ashley Ferry Town: Elements of Control in the Economic Landscape of Colonial South Carolina," *Underwater Proceedings from the Society for Historical Archaeology Conference* (1995): 88–93; Anne Simons Deas, *Recollections of the Ball Family of South Carolina (1909) and the Comingtee Plantation* (Spartenburg, S.C.: Reprint Company, 1978).

37. Henry A. M. Smith, "Childesbury," *South Carolina Historical and Genealogical Magazine* 15 (1914): 199; Caroline T. Moore and Agatha Simmons (eds.), *Abstracts of the Wills of South Carolina, 1670–1740* (Columbia, S.C.: R. L. Bryan Company, 1961), 248.

38. William Barr, "Strawberry Ferry and Childesbury Towne: A Socio-Economic Enterprise on the West Branch of the Cooper River, Berkeley County, St. Johns Parish, South Carolina," master's thesis, University of South Carolina, 1995; Barr, "Childesbury," 90.

39. Mark Newell, "The Historic Working Craft of South Carolina: A General Typology with a Study of Adaptations of Flatboat Design," Research Manuscript no.7, Georgia Archaeological Institute, Augusta, 1996, 11–12.

40. Petrona McIver, "Early Taverns of the Georgetown Road," *Names in South Carolina* 14 (Winter 1972): 33–34.

41. James Errante, "Waterscape Archaeology: A Survey for 18th-Century Boat Landings at Middleburg Plantation, Berkeley County, South Carolina," master's thesis, University of South Carolina, 1993.

42. David Beard, "Causeways and Landings: An Archaeological Study of Riverine Adaptation in South Carolina Lowcountry," in Linda F. Stine et al. (eds.), *Historic Landscapes in South Carolina: Historical Archaeological Perspectives of the Land and its People* (Charleston: Council of South Carolina Professional Archaeologists, 1993), 61–79; Theresa Hicks, "Wharves: The Keystone of Plantation Wealth? Case Studies," master's thesis, East Carolina University, 2012.

Chapter 3. Scottish Shipwrights and Shipyard Slaves

1. James Stewart was the eldest son of John, seventh laird, by his second marriage, to Margaret Finlay, sometime between 1714 and 1715.

2. James Stewart to his father, John Stewart, ca. February 1754, Shipbuilding Vertical File Collection 30-13-30, Dalguise Muniments GD38/3/6, South Carolina Historical Society. These letters are copies of documents from the Glasgow University Library Special Collection, which contains information about this shipwright.

3. James Stewart to his father, John Stewart, ca. February 1754, Shipbuilding Vertical File Collection 30-13-30, Dalguise Muniments GD38/3/6, South Carolina Historical Society. Historical records reveal that for partnerships of two European shipwrights, the partners usually who owned and operated the shipyard over time and passed on their slaves and shipyard tools to their descendants (Probate Records, *Charleston County Wills and Deeds,* 24: 963–66).

4. Jeffrey Bolster, *African American Seamen: Seafaring Work and Maritime Culture: 1750–1800*, Ph.D. diss., Johns Hopkins University, 1991; Bolster, *Black Jacks: African American Men in the Age of Sail* (Cambridge, Mass.: Harvard University Press, 1998); James Barker Farr, *Black Odyssey: The Seafaring Traditions of African Americans* (New York: Peter Lang, 1991); Marcus Rediker, *Between the Devil and the Deep Blue Sea: Merchant Seamen, Pirates and the Anglo-American World: 1700–1750* (Cambridge: Cambridge University Press, 1987); Grace Turner, "Bahamian Ship Grafitti," *International Journal of Nautical Archaeology* 35:2 (2006): 253–73.

5. As a result of the Stono Rebellion, the Assembly suspended the importation of slaves for ten years. Fears about slave revolts were prevalent among the public. Slaves,

especially boatmen, seemed to be more rebellious and were seen as threatening to the community. On January 23, 1749, Agrippa, a slave who belonged to James Akin, swore before Charles Pickney, Justice of the Peace, that many slaves from plantations along the Cooper River had plotted to seize the powder magazine in Charleston, murder the white people, and flee in pettiaugers (plantation boats) to St. Augustine. On January 24, Governor James Glen ordered the militia to apprehend the fifteen slaves and several white accomplices accused by Agrippa. After an investigation, it was concluded that the whole affair was "hellish forgery." The white men were released, but four slaves were ordered out of the province. Alexander S. Salley (ed.), *Journal of the Commons House of Assembly of South Carolina, 1748* (Columbia, S.C.: The State Company, 1907): 17. See the entry for December 20, 1748–May 18, 1749. See also Philip D. Morgan and George Terry, "Slavery in Microcosm: A Conspiracy Scare in South Carolina," *Southern Studies* 21 (1982), 121–45.

6. Henry Laurens to Thomas Savage, Charleston, November 11, 1747, in George C. Rogers Jr. et al. (eds.), *The Papers of Henry Laurens* (Columbia: University of South Carolina Press, 1972–2001), 1: 82.

7. Converse Clowse, *Economic Beginnings in Colonial South Carolina, 1670–1730* (Columbia: University of South Carolina Press, 1971), 234–35; Stuart O. Stumpf, "Implications of King George's War for the Charleston Mercantile Community," *South Carolina Historical Magazine* 77 (July, 1976): 166–88.

8. Alexander S. Salley (ed.), *Records in the British Public Office Relating to South Carolina, 1750–1751* (Columbia, S.C.: Crowson-Stone Printing Company, 1947), 24: 189–90.

9. Robert Greenhalgh Albion, *Forests and Seapower. The Timber Problem of the Royal Navy 1652–1862* (Cambridge, Mass.: Harvard University Press, 1926), 34–35, 75, 246–47.

10. Virginia Steele Wood, *Live Oaking: Southern Timber for Tall Ships* (Boston: Northeastern University Press, 1981). This book is an excellent source of detailed information about the live oaking industry for shipbuilding in the years between the Revolution and the Civil War. She uses sources such as ship records, account ledgers, personal diaries, and letters to document activities in the industry.

11. Shipworms feed on wood particles and minute particles. They do a great deal of damage to wooden ships and piers. They grow up to two feet long (60cm) and expand as they grow.

12. Marshall Smelser and William I. Davisson, "The Longevity of Colonial Ships," *American Neptune* 33:1 (January 1973): 85.

13. Ibid., 17.

14. Nicholas Olsberg, "Ship Registers in the South Carolina Archives, 1734–1780," *South Carolina and Historical and Genealogical Magazine* 74 (October 1973): 258, 266.

15. Ben Ford, "Down by the Water's Edge: Modelling Shipyard Locations in Maryland, USA," *International Journal of Nautical Archaeology* 36:1 (2007): 125–37.

16. Charles M. Andrews, *The Colonial Period of American History: England's Commercial and Colonial Policy* (New Haven: Yale University Press, 1938), 73, 77. According to the 1707 Act, a Scotsman could not trade directly with the plantations unless he resided in a colony or in England. In a colony, he could hold office, do business, and have all the advantages of an English subject. In short, Scots were almost considered English under the common law interpretation of his status; he was a king's subject. Additionally, he could serve on colonial

vessels but not English ones. Irishmen, who were initially allowed to trade under the act and who were always qualified to serve as a sailor and master, were later forbidden to have any direct connections with America. Because of the scarcity of seamen at the time, the act provided that foreigners, including Scots and Irishmen, who served two years on English ships would be considered natural-born subjects of England.

17. James Stewart to his father, John Stewart, Scotland, May 28, 1737, and August 21, 1737, Shipbuilding Vertical File 13-30-13, Dalguise Muniments GD 38/2/4, South Carolina Historical Society. Outbreaks of epidemic keratoconjunctivitis occurred among workers in shipyards and at other industrial concerns in the west of Scotland in 1956, 1967, and 1971–72. In the most recent episode, 220 persons were known to be affected; those involved were usually shipyard personnel working on the open decks of ships under construction. See D. Reid et al., "Epidemic Keratoconjunctivitis in the West of Scotland, 1967–72," *Journal of Hygiene* 73:1 (August 1974): 157–63.

18. James Stewart to his father, John Stewart, Scotland, October 17, 1749, Glasgow University Library Special Collection MS GEN 1647/1b/18. Most Scots arrived individually or in small groups from early colonial times on. Their immigration was spurred by three events: the Act of Union in 1707, which made it impossible for the Scots to advance in government, especially in the colonies; the deportation of rebel prisoners after a Jacobite uprising in 1715; and the Battle of Culloden, in 1746, after which some Scots went into exile in the Carolinas. The Scots who came to South Carolina tended to settle in Charleston, where they went into the mercantile trade or the professions.

19. James Stewart to his father, John Stewart, Scotland, May 7, 1751, Shipbuilding Vertical File 30-13-30, Dalguise Muniments GD 38/2/4, South Carolina Historical Society; James Stewart to his father, John Stewart, Scotland, October 17, 1749, Shipbuilding Vertical File 30-13-30, Dalguise Muniments GD 38/2/4, South Carolina Historical Society.

20. James Stewart to his father, John Stewart, Scotland, November 23, 1752, Shipbuilding File 30-13-30, Dalguise Muniments GD 38/2/4, South Carolina Historical Society.

21. James Stewart to his father, John Stewart, Scotland, 15 August 1752, Shipbuilding File 30-13-30, Dalguise Muniments GD 38/2/4, South Carolina Historical Society.

22. Ibid.; *South Carolina Gazette,* November 30, 1769, Shipbuilding File 30-13-30, South Carolina Historical Society.

23. George Ouchterlony, London, to James Rose, Aberdeen, June 22, 1749, Charles Irvine Collection, University of Minnesota Library, JR C/1749/4b.

24. George Ouchterlony, London, to James Rose, Aberdeen, December 13, 1748, JR C/1749/22b; John Rose, London, to Charles Irvine, Gothenberg, February 17, 1749, Charles Irvine Collection, University of Minnesota Library, CIC/1749/8a.

25. John Rose, Charleston, to Charles Irvine, Gothenburg, November 23, 1749, Charles Irvine Collection, University of Minnesota Library, CIC/1749/64a; John Rose, Charleston, to Charles Irvine, Gothenburg, January 22, 1750, Charles Irvine Collection, University of Minnesota Library, CIC/1750/6a; John Rose, Charleston, SC, to Charles Irvine, Gothenburg, November 24, 1751, Charles Irvine Collection, University of Minnesota Library CIC/1751/84a.

26. James Stewart to his father, Scotland, May 7, 1751, Shipbuilding File 30-13-30, Dalguise Muniments, GD 38/2/4, South Carolina Historical Society.

27. Henry Laurens to John Nutt, Charleston, April 25, 1757, in Rogers et al., *Laurens Papers,* 2: 532; Henry Laurens to William Cowles, June 4, 1771, in Rogers et al., *Laurens Papers,* 7: 518.

28. George Outerlony, London, to Charles Irvine, Gothenburg, November 6, 1747, Charles Irvine Collection, University of Minnesota Library, CIC/1747/17a.

29. John Rose, Charleston, to Charles Irvine, Gothenburg, July 3, 1755, Charles Irvine Collection, University of Minnesota Library, CIC/1755/27a.

30. James Rose, Aberdeen, to Charles Irvine, Gothenburg, December 6, 1755, Charles Irvine Collection, University of Minnesota Library, nra (s) 1500/ Drum/Bundle 328/item 4. 27a.

31. Henry Laurens to Reynolds, Getley and Company, Bristol, January 1, 1774, in Rogers et al., *Laurens Papers,* 9: 213. See fn. 5.

32. Under Pritchard's ownership, the property became known as Pritchard shipyard. By the time of the Revolution it was so significant a shipyard that a powder magazine and barracks were built to protect it. Pritchard leased the site to the South Carolina Navy in 1778 and 1779, before the British occupation of the city.

33. Terry Houmes and Gary Houmes, *Bubbling Spring. The Edward Kriegsmann Pritchard Family History: A Direct Line Study* (Charleston, S.C.: Professional Research Publishing Company, 1986),18.

34. U.S. Bureau of the Census, *Historical Statistics of the United States; Colonial Times to 1957,* 15 Series Z (Washington, D.C.: U.S. Bureau of the Census, 1960).

35. Records of Wills, Inventories, and Miscellaneous Records for Charleston County, South Carolina, 1671–1868, Probate Court Records, 50: 343, Charleston County Public Library, South Carolina History Collections.

36. Records of Wills, Inventories, and Miscellaneous Records for Charleston County, South Carolina, 1671–1868, Probate Court Record, June 20, 1778, Charleston County Public Library, South Carolina History Collections.

37. Henry Laurens owned the vessels named *Baker, Wambaw, Henry, Heart of Oak, Flora, Vine, Montagu, Anne,* and *Broughton Packet Island.*

38. Henry Laurens to James Grant, Charleston, September 18, 1766, in Rogers et al., *Laurens Papers,* 5: 195; Henry Laurens to Jonathan Bryan, Charleston, September 4, 176, in Rogers et al., *Laurens Papers,* 5: 291.

39. Rogers et al., *Laurens Papers,* 9: 205."Draught" means plan or design.

40. Ibid., 9: 212–17.

41. Joseph Goldenberg, *Colonial Shipbuilding* (Charlottesville: University of Virginia Press), 55–57.

42. Carl Bridenbaugh, *Colonial Craftsman* (New York: New York University Press, 1950), 93–95, 108.

43. State Site Files #38CH1038 at The South Carolina Institute of Archaeology and Anthropology, University of South Carolina.

44. Christopher F. Amer and Carleton A. Naylor, *Pritchard's Shipyard (38CH1049): Investigations of Charleston's Largest Colonial Shipyard,* Mount Pleasant, Archaeological Report, South Carolina Institute of Archaeology and Anthropology, University of South Carolina, 1996.

45. Ibid.

46. Ibid., 9.

47. Lynn Harris and Tina Rust, *Archaeological Investigations at the Hobcaw Shipyard Site, South Eastern Archaeology and History,* unpublished technical teport submitted to the State Historic Preservation Office, Charleston, S.C., 2004; L. Harris, T. Rust, and M. Beck, *Archaeological Excavations at the Hobcaw Shipyard Site, South Eastern Archaeology and History,* unpublished technical report submitted to the State Historic Preservation Office, Charleston, S.C., 2005.

48. Martha Zierden, Leslie Drucker, and Jeanne Calhoun, *Home Upriver: Rural Life on Daniel's Island, Berkley County, SC,* vol. 1, Carolina Archaeological Services, South Carolina Department of Highways and Public Transportation, 1996, esp. Figs. 3-11, 3-12, 3-13.

49. Sarah Morby, "Pritchard Shipyard: A Landscape Analysis of South Carolina's Largest Colonial and Antebellum Shipyard," master's thesis, University of South Carolina, 2000.

50. McCrady Plats Collection, Charleston County Public Library.

51. James Stewart to his father, John Stewart, Scotland, August 21, 1737, Shipbuilding Vertical File 30-13-30, Dalguise Muniments GD 38/2/4,South Carolina Historical Society.

52. Laurie Wilkie, "Glass-Knapping at a Louisiana Plantation: African American Tools," *Journal of the Society of Historical Archaeology* 30:4 (1996): 37–49.

53. Eric Poplin, "Expedient Technology in European North America; Implications of an Alternate Use of Glass by Historic Period Populations," Ph.D. diss., Archaeology Department, University of Calgary, 1986.

54. Martha Zierden, Suzanne Linder, and Ronald Anthony, "Willtown: An Archaeological and Historical Perspective." The Charleston Museum, *Archaeological Contributions* 27 (1999).

Chapter 4. From African Canoe to Carolina Crew

1. *South Carolina Gazette,* August 14, 1736; *South Carolina Gazette,* July 19, 1735; *South Carolina Gazette and Country Journal,* July 28,1772; *South Carolina Gazette and Country Journal,* July 2, 1772; *South Carolina Gazette and Country Journal,* June 11, 1771.

2. Daniel Littlefield, *Rice and Slaves: Ethnicity and the Slave Trade in Colonial South Carolina* (Baton Rouge: Louisiana State University Press, 1991), 77–78; Elizabeth Donnan (ed.), *Documents Illustrative of the History of Slave Trade* (Washington, DC: Carnegie Institute, 1930), 2: 476.

3. Catherine Coquery-Vidrovitch and Paul Lovejoy (eds.), *The Workers of the African Trade* (Beverly Hills, Calif.: Sage, 1985), 25–50.

4. John Biggers, *The Web of Life in Africa* (Austin: University of Texas Press, 1996), 35–36. This work contains several interesting contemporary drawings of canoes and fishermen. Refer to chapter 2 for more information on African boating background.

5. Thomas J. Hutchinson, *Ten Years of Wanderings amongst the Ethiopians: With Sketches of the Manners, Customs, of Civilized and Uncivilized Tribes from Senegal to Gaboon* (London: Hurst and Blacket, 1861), 50. Hutchinson (1802–1885), who was born in Ireland and settled in England, was a diplomat, physician, and travel writer. He was a fellow of the Ethnological Society, a member of the Royal Society of Literature, and Her Majesty's

Consul for the Bight of Biafra and the island of Fernando Po. He traveled in Africa from 1865 to 1861.

6. Ibid., 227–28.

7. Ibid., 247; James Holman, *Travels in Madeira, Sierra Leone, Teneriffe, St. Jago, Cape Coast, Fenando Po, Princes Island Etc. Etc.* (London: George Routledge, Leicester Square, 1840), 193. James Holman (1786–1857) was born in Exeter. Although he was afflicted by debilitating health problems, he traveled extensively and fought against the slave trade in Africa. He was elected a fellow of the British Royal Society and of the Linaean Society. Charles Darwin frequently cited his work. The Holman River in Fernandino Po was named after him. James Holman was unequivocal about his first and deepest dream. "I have been conscious from my earliest youth of the existence of this desire to explore distant regions," he would recall, "to trace the variety exhibited by mankind under different influences of different climates, customs and law."

8. Holman, *Travels in Madeira*, 229.

9. Ibid.

10. Ibid., 251.

11. Roger Smith, "The Canoe in West African History," *Journal of African History* 11:4 (1970): 518.

12. Ibid., 525–31.

13. Ibid., 520.

14. Jennifer Speake, *Literature of Travel and Exploration*, 3 vols. (New York: Taylor and Francis, 2003). Entries describe journeys, voyages, and routes; world travelers and their writings in diaries, letters, logbooks, and postcards; remarkable destinations; geographers and cartographers; and contemporary travel writers and their works. Author entries include biographical profiles. Each entry is complete with a list of references and further readings.

15. Smith, "The Canoe," 520.

16. Ibid., 523.

17. Thomas Astley (ed.), *Voyages and Travels* (London: Frank Cass and Company, 1968), 2: 252.

18. Ibid., 2: 202. Zacharias Taurinius, *Travels through the interior of Africa, from the Cape of Good Hope to Morocco; in Caffraria, the Kingdoms of Mataman, Angola, Massi, Monoemugi, Muschako, Bahahara, Wangara, Haoussa, & c., &c. and thence through the desert of Sahara and the north of Barbary to Morocco. Between the years 1781 and 1797* (London: R. Philips, 1801), 407, 502; Edmund James Web (ed.), *Africa as Seen by the Explorers* (London: E. Arnold, 1899),123–24.

19. Astley, *Travels,* 3: 650

20. Astley, *Travels,* 3: 266, 650. This section discusses the Gold Coast voyages of Jean Barbot.

21. Ibid., 243.

22. Ibid., 651.

23. Ibid., 650.

24. Ibid., 650.

25. Holman, *Travels in Madeira,* 195, 347.

26. Astley, *Travels,* 4: 382.

27. Ibid., 195–203.

28. Kevin Dawson, "Enslaved Swimmers and Divers in the Atlantic World," *Journal of American History,* 92:4 (2006):1320–55; Pieter de Marees, *Description and Historical Account of the Gold Kingdom of Guinea,* trans. Albert van Dantzig and Adam Jones (1602; New York: Hakluyt Society, 1987), 26, 32; *Pieter van der Broecke's Journal of Voyages to Cape Verde, Guinea, and Angola,* 1605–1612, trans. J. D. La Fleur (1634; London: Hakluyt Society, 2000), 37; Horatio Bridge, *Journal of an African Cruiser: Comprising Sketches of the Canaries, the Cape Verdes, Liberia, Madeira, Sierra Leone, and other places of Interest on the West Coast of Africa* (New York: Wiley and Putnam, 1845); Hair, Jones, and Law (eds.), *Barbot on Guinea,* II, 532.

29. R. S. Rattray, *Ashanti* (Oxford: Oxford University Press, 1963), 63–65; Mungo Park, *Travels in the Interior Districts of Africa: Performed under the Direct Patronage of the African Association the Years 1795, 1796, and 1797* (1799; New York: Arno Press, 1971), 71–72, 210–11.

30. D. O. Dapper, *Description de l'Afrique . . . Traduite du Flamand* (Description of Africa . . . translated from Dutch) (Amsterdam: Chez Wolfang, Waesberge, Boom & van Someren, 1970).

31. Rattray, *Ashanti,* 63–65; De Marees, *Description and Historical Account of the Gold Kingdom,* 186–87.

32. Web, *Africa as Seen by its Explorers,* 130–31.

33. Astley, *Travels,* 2: 183.

34. Peter Breunig, "The 8000-Year-Old Dugout Canoe from Dufuna (NE Nigeria)," in G. Pwiti and R. Soper (eds.), *Aspects of African Archaeology.* Papers from the Tenth Congress of the Pan-African Association for Prehistory and Related Studies (Harare: University of Zimbabwe Publications, 1996), 461–68.

35. Jojada Verrips, "Ghaniain Canoe Decorations," *Maritime Studies* 1:1 (2002): 43–66. *Maritime Studies* (MAST) is a good source of articles about traditional fishing boats and fishing communities (http://www.marecentre.nl/mast/backissues.html). See also Allison Winnifred Gray, "Canoe Decoration and Meaning amongst the Fante of the Cape Coast," *African Diaspora Collection,* School for International Training (SIT), Graduate Institute/SIT Study Abroad, 1996.

Chapter 5. The Plantation Patroon

1. Lawrence Levine, *Black Culture and Consciousness: Afro-American Folk Thought from Slavery to Freedom* (New York: Oxford University Press, 1977), 12. This is an interesting compilation of folklore documents containing many quotations from songs, jokes, and stories, which the author uses to try to communicate a sense of black thought.

2. Edward McCrady, *The History of South Carolina under the Royal Government, 1719–1776* (New York: Macmillin Company, 1899), 516.

3. *South Carolina Gazette,* April 6, 1734; April 11, 1739; January 1, 1743. "Patroon" is a West Indies term denoting captain of a boat.

4. *South Carolina Gazette and General Advertiser,* April 10–13, 1784.

5. *Royal Gazette,* September 21–28, 1782.

6. *South Carolina Gazette,* September 14–21, 1767.

7. *South Carolina and American General Gazette,* April 10, 1777.

8. William Howard Russel, *My Diary North and South* (New York: Harper, 1863), 58.

9. Samuel Gaillard Stoney and William John Grayson, "The Autobiography of William John Grayson," *South Carolina Historical and Genealogical Magazine* 49 (January 1948): 25.

10. Levine, *Black Culture and Black Consciousness*, 12.

11. Robert M. Weir, *Colonial South Carolina* (Millwood, N.Y.: KTO Press, 1983), 181. While this study does not explore the academic discourse pertaining to slaves and resistance; boat slaves who ran away, stole boats, or served as a communication network along the waterways could be discussed as an integral part of this theme. Historians have grappled with the concepts of rebellion and resistance by slaves in the American South with the development of the everyday resistance models in the 1960s and with continued work to the present. Part of the analytical process involved developing clear definitions of types of resistance as well as determining the effects of resistance. To some historians, this was limited to a question of violent uprisings, such as those carried out by Nat Turner and Denmark Vesey. To others, the question was not strictly one of overt actions on a large scale but included small-scale or everyday actions that undermined the ability of whites to shape slaves' ideologies and behavior to their liking. Breaking tools, working slowly, feigning illness, stealing, and running away in small groups or as individuals were all acts of resistance that elicited changes in the slave regime or inhibited the successful attainment of a slave owner's economic goals. Among other sources see Herbert Aptheker, *American Negro Slave Revolts* (New York: Columbia University Press, 1943); Eugene Genovese, "Rebelliousness and Docility in the Negro Slave," *Civil War History* 13 (December 1967).

12. "The Petition of Merchants, Traders, Planters, and Other Interested in the Trade and Prosperity of South Carolina and Georgia," December 21, 1756, in George C. Rogers Jr. et al. (eds.), *The Papers of Henry Laurens* (Columbia: University of South Carolina Press, 1972–2001), 2: 379.

13. Henry Laurens to John Loveday, Camden, June 21, 1777, in Rogers et al., *Laurens Papers*, 11: 384–87.

14. Henry Laurens to Timothy Creamer, Charleston, June 26, 1774, in Rogers et al., *Laurens Papers*, 4: 319.

15. Henry Laurens to John Smith, Charleston, May 30, 1765, in Rogers et al., *Laurens Papers*, 4: 633.

16. Names of boatmen that appear in the Henry Laurens records include Abraham, Achilles, Cuffee, Pompey, Scaramouch, Tom Peas, Jemmy, and Sampson.

17. Henry Laurens to Captain George Dick, Charleston, June 1964, in Rogers et al., *Laurens Papers*, 4: 298–300.

18. Henry Laurens to John Smith, Charleston, March 11, 1766, in Rogers et al., *Laurens Papers*, 5: 86; Henry Laurens to John Hopton, September 4, 1771, in Rogers et al., *Laurens Papers* 7: 566, 573; Henry Laurens to John Smith, February 4, 1766, in Rogers et al., *Laurens Papers*, 5: 67; Henry Laurens to James Penman, Charleston, October 13, 1767, in Rogers et al., *Laurens Papers* 5: 353–55.

19. Alexander S. Salley, *Journal of the Commons House of Assembly of South Carolina, 1745–1756* (Columbia, S.C.: The State Company, 1932), 556.

20. Henry Laurens to Alexander Tweed, October 11, 1765, in Rogers et al., *Laurens Papers*, 5: 23; Thomas Cooper and David James McCord (eds.), *The Statutes at Large of South*

Carolina (Columbia, S.C.: A. S. Johnston, 1836–1841), 7: 409. Slaves were prohibited from keeping boats, canoes, or perriaugers.

21. *South Carolina Gazette,* April 3, 1762; Robert Raper Letterbook, Raper to Colleton, May 22, 1760, South Carolina Historical Society, Collection.

22. Affidavit to Lord Charles Greenville Montagu signed by John Wragg, Berkeley County, South Carolina, in Rogers et al., *Laurens Papers,* 5: 427; Permit or Sufference for 6 Months, May 14, 1767, in Rogers et al., *Laurens Papers,* 5: 225in; Henry Laurens to James Haberham, Charleston, September 5, 1767, in Rogers et al., *Laurens Papers* 5: 292–99. Contains a description of how a pass was given out by a Collector for a slave patroon named Jemmy for an extra dollar.

23. Main components in the colonial carrying trade leaving the port of Charleston from 1740 to1766 are listed as rice, naval stores, deerskins, indigo, staves, lumber, corn and peas, tanned leather, beef and pork, silk, tallow, cotton, and hemp. See Thomas Papers, 11/419/10 South Carolina Historical Society, for numerous listings of import/export shipping trends at Charleston's port.

24. Roy Merrens, *The Colonial South Carolina Scene* (Columbia: University of South Carolina Press, 1977), 181; Converse Clowse, *Economic Beginnings in Colonial South Carolina, 1670–1730* (Columbia: University of South Carolina Press, 1971); Stuart O. Stumpf, "Implications of King Georges War for the Charleston Mercantile Community," *South Carolina Historical Magazine* 77 (July, 1976): 161–88. In 1706, sixty- eight inward-bound vessels crossed the harbor bar; in 1715, 133 sails entered; in 1735 there were 248 entries; by 1755, there were 300 entries; and in the decade prior to the Revolution between 450 and 500 ships called at Charleston annually. There was also a steady growth in the size of vessels. The 1717 average was forty-six tons per vessel; this had increased to 133 tons by 1777.

25. Ibid., 7: 231–32.

26. *South Carolina Gazette,* April 27– May 4, 1734.

27. *South Carolina Gazette,* July 1–8, 1732.

28. *South Carolina Gazette,* December 1–3, 1737.

29. *South Carolina Gazette,* July 25–August 1, 1740; February 19–26, 1741.

30. *South Carolina Gazette,* February 16, 1769.

31. *South Carolina Gazette,* March 30, 1752.

32. *South Carolina Gazette,* March 23–30, 1738.

33. Craig Marin, "Following the Water: The Resistance Activities of Slave Boatmen in South Carolina and Georgia, 1732–1800," master's thesis, University of Pittsburgh, 1998, 9–11. Also see Lathan Windley's compilation of advertisements found in surviving newspapers from the period: *Runaway Slave Advertisements: A Documentary History from the 1730s to 1790* (Westport, Conn.: Greenwood Press, 1983). For numbers of skilled runaways and male runaways, see Lathan Windley, *A Profile of Runaway Slaves in Virginia and South Carolina from 1730 through 1787* (New York: Garland Press, 1995), 171–73.

34. Alexander S. Salley, *Records in British Public Office Relating to South Carolina* (Columbia: Historical Commission of South Carolina, 1928–1946), 14: 124–25; "Dom Rex versus Three Negroe Slaves," July 28, 1737, Microfilm Reel 2 1736–1738, *Admiralty Court Records,* South Carolina Department of Archives and History.

35. "An Act to Prevent the Inveigling, Stealing, and Carrying Away Negroes and other slaves in this province giving Freedom to a Negro man named Arrah belonging to Mr.

Hugh Cartwright. No.754. June 13, 1747," in Cooper and McCord, *Statutes*, 7: 419–20. Many of the advertisements for runaways who had sailing experience or were "brought up to the sea" expressed the masters' concerns that they might try to pass as free. This concern was not evidenced in cases where the slave in question did not have oceangoing experience. This suggests that masters made skill distinctions between sailors and boatmen and that free blacks were restricted from or chose not to engage in river and local coastal work.

36. *A Collection of Voyages*, 1: 33.

37. David Wiggins, "Leisure Time on Southern Plantations: The Slaves Respite from Constant Toil, 1810–1860," in Donald Spivey (ed.), *Sport in America: New Historical Perspectives* (Westport, Conn.: Greenwood Press, 1985), 37.

38. J. G. Clinkscales, *On the Old Plantation: Reminiscences of His Childhood* (New York: Band and White, 1916), 7–9, 26–29, 35–36; Lignon, *True and Exact History of the Island of Barbadoes,* (Cambridge, Mass.: Hackett Publishing, 2011), 52–53; David Wiggins, "Good Times on the Ol' Plantation: Popular Recreations of the Black Slave in the Antebellum South, 1810–1860," *Journal of Sport History* 4:3 (1997): 273–74; Richard Mandell, *Sport: A Cultural History* (New York: 1984), 112–13, 179–80; Eugene D. Genovese, *Roll Jordan Roll: The World the Slaves Made,* vol. 652 (New York: Random House Digital, 1972), 569.

39. Clinkscales, *On the Old Plantation,* 7–9, 26–29, 35–36.

40. John Lawson, *A New Voyage to South Carolina* (Chapel Hill: University of North Carolina Press, 1967), 140.

41. William Elliot, *Carolina Sports by Land and Water: Including Incidents of Devil Fishing, Wild-Cat, Deer, and Bear Hunting Etc.* (1859; Columbia, S.C.: Derby and Jackson, 1994); Walter Edgar, *South Carolina: A History* (Columbia: University of South Carolina Press, 1998), 155; Ambrose Gonzales, *The Black Border: Gullah Stories of the Carolina Coast* (Columbia, S.C.: Applewood Books's Store, 2010), 121–24; Janet Shaw, *Journal of a Lady of Quality: Being the Narrative of a Journey from Scotland to the West Indies, North Carolina and Portugal, in the years 1774–1776,* ed. Evangeline Walker Andrews (New Haven: University of Nebraska Press, 1934), 121–12; Robert Q. Mallard, *Plantation Life before Emancipation* (Richmond, Va.: Negro History Press, 1892).

42. Mallard, *Plantation Life*, 21–28.

43. Ibid., 27.

44. *South Carolina Gazette,* November 5, 1737; Philip Morgan, *Slave Counterpoint: Black Culture in the Eighteenth-Century Chesapeake and Lowcountry* (Chapel Hill: University of North Carolina Press, 1998), 240–41; Robert Olwell, *Masters, Slaves, and Subjects: The Culture of Power in the South Carolina Lowcountry, 1740–1790* (Ithaca, N.Y.: Cornell University Press, 1998).

45. Peter Wood, *Black Majority: Negroes in South Carolina from 1670 through the Stono Rebellion.* (New York: W. W. Norton, 1974), 201.

46. *South Carolina Gazette,* September 24, 1772: November 18, 1780.

47. Morgan, *Slave Counterpoint,* 241.

48. *South Carolina Gazette,* September 24, 1772; Records of Wills, Inventories, and Miscellaneous Records for Charleston County, South Carolina, Charleston County Public Library, South Carolina History Collections, Inventory Book Y, 306–7. See the Inventory of Daniel Chopard, August 3, 1770, and his estate; *South Carolina Gazette,* August 30, 1770.

49. Carroll Quigley, "Aboriginal Fish Poisons and Diffusion Problem," *American Anthropologist* 58 (1956): 508–25; Cooper and McCord, *Statutes,* 3: 170.

50. Morgan, *Counterpoint,* 138; Wood, *Black Majority,* 122–23; Kate Singleton (ed.), "Archaeological Evidence for Subsistance on the Coastal Plantations," in *The Archaeology of Slavery* (Orlando, Fla.: Academic Press, 1985), 163–91.

51. Lucius G. Moffatt and Joseph M. Carriere (eds.), "A Frenchman Visits Charleston, 1817," *South Carolina Historical and Genealogical Magazine* 49 (1948): 136.

52. Wood, *Black Majority,* 116–17, 201.

53. *South Carolina Gazette,* March 12, 1744; June 10, 1745; December 2, 1732. These issues contain notices listing skills of slaves as boatbuilders and ship carpenters.

54. Malcolm Bell Jr., *Major Butler's Legacy: Five Generations of a Slaveholding Family* (Athens: University of Georgia Press, 1987), 116–17.

55. Mary Allison Carrill, "The Role of the Black Artisan in the Building Trades and Decorative Arts of the South," Ph.D. diss., Columbia University, 1982, 131. Much of her information was derived from the *South Carolina Gazette* and the *City Gazette and Daily Advertizer.*

56. Ibid., 218–19.

57. *South Carolina Gazette,* April 27, 1738.

58. Joseph Goldenberg, *Shipbuilding in Colonial America* (Charlottesville: University of Virginia Press), 66–67.

59. James Harold Easterby et al. (eds.), *Journals of the Commons House of Assembly, 1671–1775* (Columbia: Historical Commission of South Carolina, 1951–1983), 541, 547. These pages contain acts, resolutions, and discussions relevant to shipbuilding.

60. Goldenberg, *Colonial Shipbuilding,* 64–65; Leonard Price Stavisky, "The Negro Artisan in the South Atlantic States, 1800–1860: A Study of Status and Economic Opportunity with Special Reference to Charleston," Ph.D. diss., Columbia University, 1958, 7. These eighteenth-century problems continued into the nineteenth century, and the slave owners' arguments in these petitions were turned into arguments against them by antislavery activists, who argued against the use of black laborers in industry because they believed that slavery discouraged the arts, and manufacturers argued that protecting slave labor prevented the importation of white laborers "who enrich and strengthen a country," appearing to relate to humanitarian concerns for white immigrants. Employers also considered the effects of mechanical training on a slave, who, with a modicum of education, could become a dangerous person. Mastering a craft could make him resentful of his status and complicate further his subjugation. Furthermore, access to a craftsman's tools might provide him with weapons.

61. William Pease and Jane Pease, *The Web of Progress: Private Values and Public Styles in Boston and Charleston, 1828–1843* (New York: Oxford University Press, 1985), 45.

62. See Occupational Distribution of Charleston Males according Race and Nativity in the Mid-1800s, tabulated in Bernard E. Powers, *Black Charlestonians: A Social History, 1822–1885* (Fayetteville: University of Arkansas Press, 1994).

63. David Smith, "Dependent Urbanization in Colonial America: The Case of Charleston South Carolina," *Social Forces* 66:1 (September 1987): 19.

64. Lynn Harris, "Public Education and Submerged Small Craft Documentation in South Carolina," *Museum Small Craft Transactions* 3 (1996–1997): 46–54.

Chapter 6. Fair Winds, Fair Trade and Fair Due

1. Thomas Cooper and David J. McCord, *The Statutes at Large of South Carolina* (Columbia, S. C.: A. S. Johnson, 1840), 434–30 (1796 Law), 454–55 (1817 Law); 265–66 (1825 Law), 529 (1835 Law). Loren Schweniger, "Slave Independence and Enterprise in South Carolina, 1780–1865," *South Carolina Historical Magazine* 90:2 (April 1992): 101–25.

2. *South Carolina Gazette,* December 22, 1768.

3. *South Carolina Gazette,* March 8, 1760.

4. Petition of the Charleston Wharf Owners and Merchants to the South Carolina General Assembly, no. 1825 and no. 1895, South Carolina Department of Archives and History.

5. Walter Minchinton, "Richard Champion, Nicholas Pocock, and the Carolina Trade," *South Carolina Historical Magazine* 65 (April 1964): 87–97. The logbook of the vessel *Lloyd,* commanded by Nicholas Pocock, which traded with South Carolina from Bristol, survives in the National Maritime Museum at Greenwich, near London. Details and problems of eighteenth-century trade with Charleston are highlighted, including ship management, the need for pilotage and ballast, dependence on favorable winds, and loss of seamen through desertion. Collection MS 56/ 051, National Maritime Museum, London.

6. Alexander Salley (ed.), *Records in the British Public Office Relating to South Carolina,* (Columbia: Historical Commission of South Carolina, 1928–1947), 3: 247.

7. Ibid., 30: 247, 250, 257.

8. Ball Family Papers, Account and Blanket Book, 1720–1778, Manuscript Collection 11-515-5, South Carolina Historical Society.

9. Diaries of Charles Drayton (1784–1790), February 10, 1785, Special Collections, College of Charleston Library.

10. Walter Edgar (ed.), *The Letterbook of Robert Pringle* (Columbia: University of South Carolina Press, 1972), 116–17.

11. William H. Pease and Jane H. Pease, *The Web of Progress: Private Values and Public Styles in Boston and Charleston, 1828–1843* (New York: Oxford University Press, 1985), 40–41.

12. Edgar, *Pringle Letterbook,* 723. Also see pp. 736 and 800 for mention of ships at Childesbury.

13. *South Carolina Gazette,* June 27, 1768.

14. Leila Sellers, *Charleston Business on the Eve of the Revolution* (Chapel Hill: University of North Carolina Press, 1934), 64.

15. John Rubens Smith, "View of Charleston, South Carolina, perhaps looking southwest, showing ships, sailboats, and five men in a rowboat," Library of Congress Prints and Photographs Division, Washington, D.C., http://hdl.loc.gov/loc.pnp/pp.print; Smith, "View of Charleston, South Carolina, possibly looking north toward Sullivan's Island," Library of Congress Prints and Photographs Division, Washington, D.C., http://hdl.loc.gov/loc.pnp/pp.print.

16. *South Carolina Gazette,* January 11, 1768.

17. *South Carolina Gazette,* April 12, 1768.

18. *South Carolina Gazette,* January 25–February 1, 1768.

19. *South Carolina Gazette,* July 9–16, 1763.

20. Howard Chapelle, *The History of American Sailing Ships* (New York: Bonanza Books, 1935), 11.

21. William Fleetwood, *Tidecraft: The Boats of South Carolina, Georgia and Northeastern Florida, 1550–1950* (Tybee Island, Ga.: W.B.G. Marine Press, 1995), 51.

22. William Baker, *Sloops and Shallops* (Columbia: University of South Carolina Press, 1966), 119. It should be noted that this trend represents only registered vessels involved in the intercolonial trade, not those nonregistered vessels (e.g., canoes and periaguas) used in coastal and inland trade and transportation. These may have had sloop rigs and removable masts.

23. Edward Charles Lesnick, "A Quantitative Analysis of the Supply and Demand for Ships: A Case Study of Colonial New York and Carolina," Ph.D. diss., University of Notre Dame, 1973, 151, 158, 161, 209, 210. This dissertation is a comparative quantitative study of the shipbuilding and shipping industries of the eighteenth-century colonies of New York and South Carolina. The author attempts to compare economic performance and the impact of maritime industries on regional growth and development in a northern and a southern colony. Lesnick's work tests certain hypotheses by statistical methods. His data comprise statistics about supply and demand for shipping. He looks at variables such as vessel rig, tonnage, crew size, and construction details.

24. Henry Laurens to Charles Crokatt, Charleston, June11 , 1764, in George C. Rogers Jr. et al., *The Papers of Henry Laurens* (Columbia: University of South Carolina Press, 1972–2001), 4: 306.

25. Henry Laurens was assisting Oswald from London in establishing a plantation in the backcountry of South Carolina, as well providing advice about necessary accessories such as boats.

26. Henry Laurens to Richard Oswald, October 10, 1764, in Rogers et al., *Laurens Papers* 4: 465–66.

27. Chapman Milling, *Colonial South Carolina* (Columbia: University of South Carolina Press, 1951), 91–92. "A Description of South Carolina," by Governor James Glen, is reprinted in this work.

28. Firewood was in demand not only by local families but also by ships that put into port.

29. Sellers, *Charleston Business*, 86.

30. Strawberry Ferry Ledger, in Rogers et al., *Laurens Papers*, 11: 594–95, Appendix A. This is a two-page account kept by Lancelot Smith from 1777 to 1779 for Henry Laurens.

31. Henry Laurens Ledger, 1766–1773, Special Collections, College of Charleston Library.

32. Henry Laurens to Richard Oswald, Charleston, July 7, 1764, in Rogers et al., *Laurens Papers*, 4: 338.

33. Ulrich Bonnel Philips, "The Slave Labor Problem in the Charleston District," *Political Science Quarterly* 22:3 (September 1907): 416–39.

34. Henry Laurens to Richard Oswald, Charleston, October 16, 1767, in Rogers et al., *Laurens Papers*, 5: 379.

35. Henry Laurens to Joseph Brown, Charleston, July 24, 1765, in Rogers et al., *Laurens Papers*, 4: 658.

36. Henry Laurens Ledger, Special Collections, College of Charleston Library. As planters were co-owners of ships, payment for cargoes, seamen and captain's wages, porterage, wharfage, and stowage constituted a complicated process that involved fractional costs. Laurens Ledger, October 1766, lists his share of costs for the *Heart of Oak,* the *Flora,* the *Vine,* and the *Henry.*

37. Sellers, *Charleston Business,* 67; Sylvia R. Frey, *Water from the Rock: Black Resistance in a Revolutionary Age* (Princeton: Princetown University Press, 1991); Lathan Windley (ed.), *Runaway Slave Advertisements: A Documentary History from the 1730s to 1790s* (Westport, Conn.: Greenwood Press 1983), 1: 477.

38. Petition of Benjamin Webb, James Anderson, et al. to the South Carolina General Assembly, 1785, no. 100, South Carolina Department of Archives and History; Petition of Nathaniel Heyward, John Gibbes, Daniel Blake, and Anne Gibbes to the South Carolina General Assembly, 1806, no. 92, South Carolina Department of Archives and History; Richard Dawson, William Buckner, Isaac Taylor, et. al. (Beaufort District) to the South Carolina General Assembly, South Carolina Department of Archives and History.

39. Charles Ball, *Slavery in the United States: A Narrative of the Life and Adventures of Charles Ball, a Black Man* (Detroit: Negro History Press, 1970), 232–33.

40. Windley, *Slave Advertisements,* 341; Philip Morgan, *Slave Counterpoint: Black Culture in the Eighteenth-Century Chesapeake and Lowcountry* (Chapel Hill: University of North Carolina Press, 1998), 64; *South Carolina Gazette,* July 27, 1784.

41. Edgar, *Pringle Letterbook,* 173, 471, 490–92, 566, 777; Laurens Ledger, Special Collections, College of Charleston Library.

42. Laurens Ledger. It is not evident how long this voyage lasted, as part of this document is missing.

43. Edgar, *Pringle Letterbook,* 490.

44. Governor Parry of Barbadoes wrote to the colonial office in 1786 that "the numbers of Negroe slaves employed in Navigating the Trading Vessels in these seas (particularly the Bermuda's) seem to me to increase so much as to require the attention of the British legislature, as it throws so many English seamen out of employment." Also see Jarvis, Michael J. "Maritime Masters and Seafaring Slaves in Bermuda, 1680-1783." The William and Mary Quarterly 59.3 (2002): 585-622.

45. Marcus Rediker, *Between the Devil and the Deep Blue Sea: Merchant Seamen, Pirates, and the Anglo-American World, 1700–1750* (Cambridge: Cambridge University Press, 1987), 56; South Carolina Admiralty Records, Charleston County Library. For an example of a well-documented case heard in the South Carolina Admiralty Courts in Charleston, see the charges brought against his mutinous crew by John Clipperton, master of the slave ship *Hannah Succession* in *Clipperton vs Seamen,* 494–95, South Carolina Admiralty Records, Charleston County Library.

46. Jesse Lemisch, "Jack Tar in the Streets: Merchant Seamen in the Politics of Revolutionary America," *William and Mary Quarterly* 3:25 (1968): 378–80; Cooper and McCord, *The Statutes,* 3: 735–36.

47. Linebaugh and Rediker, *Between the Devil,* 233. The most common description of a mob in revolutionary America was a "Rabble of boys, sailors, and Negroes" (228).

48. Ibid., 226; Henry Laurens to John Laurens, Charleston, June 18 and 25, 1775, in Rogers et al., *Laurens Papers,* 10: 184, 191.

49. Ship Registers 1765–1774, South Carolina Department of Archives and History.

50. Leonard Woods Labaree (ed.), *Royal Instructions to the British Colonial Governors, 1670–1776* (New York: Octagon Books, 1967), 887. The first set of colonial trade instructions was prepared in 1685 by the Lords of Trade with the assistance of the Commissioners of Customs. The instructions were submitted by them to the Lords of Treasury and then referred to the Board of Trade for comment. Each newly appointed governor received a set of these instructions. Often no copy of trade instructions to a particular governor is available. Gaps in the information are most prevalent for the years 1755–1766. In other cases, clerks in the Plantation office did not copy the instructions in full.

51. Ibid., 2: 885–905. "Governor Glen to Lord Commissioners for Trade and Plantations, South Carolina," March 1753, contains his observations about shipping trade instructions, regulations for naval officers, and aspects of the Navigation Acts.

52. Labaree, *Royal Instructions,* 2:766.

53. Cooper and McCord, *Statutes,* 4: 109–11,170–75.

54. Henry Laurens to Ross and Mill, Charleston, October 31, 1769, in Rogers et al., *Laurens Papers,* 7: 188.

55. Henry Laurens to Richard Grubb, Charleston, March 4, 1769, in Rogers et al., *Laurens Papers,* 6: 400.

56. Salley, *British Records,* 31: 273. Custom houses were located in Charleston, Beaufort, and Georgetown. It was not until January 1766 that Charles Garth, gent for South Carolina, presented a memorial to the Board of Trade regarding this issue.

57. There is an account of the plantation products that Henry Laurens supplied to the Georgia government between April 6, 1776, and July 2, 1777, in Rogers et al., *Laurens Papers,* 11: 596–97.

58. Sellers, *Charleston Business,* 194–97. Laurens had to pay all the costs of the suit against him, includinga judge's fee of £277 and £175 to repurchase his vessel. Another vessel belonging to Laurens, the *Broughton Island,* was also on trial at the same time for an incident involving ballast logs that the customs officials declared as a cargo; Laurens was charged with not having a lumber bond.

59. Rogers et al., *Laurens Papers,* 7: xv–xvi.

60. Alexander Salley (ed.), *Journals of the Commissioners of the Navy of South Carolina, 9 October 1769 to March 1 16 1779* (Columbia, S.C.: The State Company, 1912), 193.

61. Ibid.

62. Ibid., 1577.

63. Leonard Price Stavisky, "The Negro Artisan in the South Atlantic States, 1800–1860: A Study of Status and Economic Opportunity with Special Reference to Charleston," Ph.D. diss., Columbia University, 1958, 22; J. B. Easterby (ed.), *The South Carolina Rice Plantation as Revealed by the Papers of Robert F. W. Alston* (Columbia: University of South Carolina Press, 2004), revised publication, 388; Frederick P. Bowes, *The Culture of Early Charleston* (Chapel Hill: University of North Carolina Press, 1942), 113; *South Carolina Gazette,* February 13, 1861.

64. Leonard Price Stavisky, "The Negro Artisan in the South Atlantic States, 1800–1860: A Study of Status and Economic Opportunity with Special Reference to Charleston," Ph.D. diss., Columbia University, 1958, 22

65. Robert Q. Mallard, *Plantation Life before Emancipation* (Richmond, Va.: Negro History Press, 1892), 202. *South Carolina Gazette,* February 13, 1861. For pro-slavery arguments see sources of information such as newspaper articles about the value of slaves and how the "loss" of the institution of slavery would be a detriment to the South, especially Charleston, where slaves were being shifted from the rice culture.

66. Christopher Amer et al. "The Malcolm Boat (38BK803): Discovery Stabilization, and Preservation of a Historic Seagoing Smallcraft in the Ashley River," Research Manuscript no. 217, South Carolina Institute of Archaeology and Anthropology, University of South Carolina, Columbia, 1997.

67. Frederick M. Hocker, "The Place of the Brown's Ferry Vessel in the Evolution of the Flat Bottomed Boat," Texas A&M University, College Station, 1985.

68. Ibid. See also Frederick M. Hocker, "The Brown's Ferry Vessel: An Interim Hull Report," *Underwater Archaeology Proceedings from the Society for Historical Archaeology Conference* (1992): 20–25.

69. Frederick M. Hocker, "The Brown's Ferry Vessel: An Interim Hull Report," Frederick M. Hocker, "The Clydesdale Plantation Project Report: 1992 Field Report," *Institute for Nautical Archaeology Quarterly* 19:4 (1992): 12–16.

70. Susan Lynn Vezeau, "The Mepkin Abbey Shipwreck: Diving into South Carolina's Plantation Past," master's thesis, Anthropology Department, Texas A&M University, 2004.

71. Harry Pecorelli III, "Archaeological Investigations of the B&B Plantation Wreck (38BK1762): An Eighteenth-Century Plantation Vessel, Charleston, South Carolina," master's thesis, History Department, East Carolina University, 2003.

A Final Note. A CANOW *Missing!* A CANOE *Found!* A PETTIAGER *Lives On!*

1. Daniel Brown, Kathryn Cooper, and Lynn Harris, "The Plantation Boat *Accommodation:* The Historical and Archaeological Investigation of the Maritime Icon of the South, Part 1," *Nautical Research Journal* 56:2 (Summer 2011): 93–114.

2. http://beaufortartist.blogspot.com/2007/10/periauger.html (accessed May 20, 2012); http://www.ncpublications.com/comments/ccOct04.pdf (accessed May 20, 2012); http://www.continentalline.org/articles/0001/000101.htm (accessed May 20, 2012).

Bibliography

Primary Sources

Archival Collections and Manuscripts

Charleston County Public Library, South Carolina History Collections
  Records of Wills, Inventories, and Miscellaneous Records for Charleston County, South Carolina, 1671–1868
Charleston County Register of Mesne Conveyance
  McCrady Historic Plat Collection
Charleston Museum
  Photograph Collection
  Exhibit boats: Acommodation and Bessie
College of Charleston Library, Special Collections
  British Public Record Office documents, 5 volumes, and microfilm, 31 reels
  Henry Laurens Ledger
South Carolina Department of Archives and History, Columbia
  Admiralty Court Records, 1736–1738
  Ship Registers, 1734–1780, 2 volumes
  Vice Admiralty Court Journals, 1716–1763, microfilm, 3 reels
South Carolina Historical Society, Charleston
  Ball Family Papers, Account and Blanket Book, 1720–1778
  Collection 11/515
  Ball Family Collection, 1776–1840, Collection 11/515516
  British Public Record Office documents, 1716–1776, Collection 3469/74
  Commissioner of Trade and Plantations Documents, 1719–740
  Dunlap, William, Correspondence and Muniments, 1685–ca.1690, microfilm, 1 reel
  Laurens, Henry 1724–1792, Collection 37
  Locke, John, correspondence, 1673–1704, microfilm, 1 reel
  Shaftesbury Papers, 1663–1712, microfilm, 3 reels
  Shipbuilding File, Collection 30-13-30
South Caroliniana Library, University of South Carolina, Manuscript Collections
  Charleston Account Books, Collection 389.198

James Ford Bell Library, University of Minnesota
Irvine Collection, correspondence of John Rose, Jams Rose, George Ouchterlony, and Charles Irvine
Library of Congress Prints and Photographs Division, Washington, D.C.
John Rubens Smith artwork
The Atlantic Slave Trade and Slave Life in the Americas: A Visual Record
University of Virginia
http://hitchcock.itc.virginia.edu/Slavery/index.php (This site provides a collection of images related to American slave trade and slave societies. The images were compiled from a variety of sources and consist primarily of visual documents dating to the period of slavery. The exhibit is sponsored by the Virginia Foundation for the Humanities and by the Digital Media Lab at the University of Virginia.)
Periauger Project in North Carolina website, http://beaufortartist.blogspot.com/2007/10/periauger.html

Newspapers

Georgia Gazette, 1763–1770. Savannah: James Johnson, publisher.
South Carolina and American General Gazette, 1764–1781, microfilm, 12 reels. Charleston: Robert Wells and David Bruce, publishers.
South Carolina Gazette, 1732–1776, microfilm, 12 reels. Charleston: Peter Timothy, publisher.
South Carolina Gazette and Country Journal, 1765–1775, microfilm, 12 reels. Charleston: Charles Crouch, publisher.
South Carolina Gazette.

Published Primary Materials and Public Records

Astley, Thomas, ed. *Voyages and Travels.* 4 vols. London: Frank Cass and Company, 1968.
Ball, Charles. *Slavery in the United States: A Narrative of the Life and Adventures of Charles Ball, A Black Man*. Detroit, Mich.: Negro History Press, 1970.
Bartram, William. *Travels and Other Writings. Travels through North and South Carolina, Georgia East and West Florida, 1773–1774*. Savannah: Beehive Press, 1973.
Basye, Arthur H., ed. *The Lords Commissioners of Trade and Plantations, Commonly Known as the Board of Trade, 1748–1772*. New Haven: Yale University Press, 1925.
Bridge, Horatio. *Journal of an African Cruiser: Comprising Sketches of the Canaries, the Cape Verdes, Liberia, Madeira, Sierra Leone, and other places of Interest on the West Coast of Africa*. New York: Wiley and Putnam, 1845.
Cheves, Langdon, ed. *Shaftesbury Papers.* Collections of the South Carolina Historical Society, Charleston, 1897.
Clinkscales, J. G. *On the Old Plantation: Reminiscences of his Childhood.* New York: Negro Universities Press, 1916.
Cooper, Thomas, and David J. McCord, eds. *The Statutes at Large of South Carolina.* 10 vols. Columbia, S.C.: A. S. Johnston, 1836–1841.Dapper, Olfert. *Description de l'Afrique . . . Traduite du Flamand* [Description of Africa. . .]. Translated from Dutch, 1668; Amsterdam, 1686.
Da Silva, Augusto Epifanio, ed. *Esmeraldo de Situ Orbis.* Lisbon: Sociedade de Geografia de Lisboa,1975.

De Marees, Pieter. *Description and Historical Account of the Gold Kingdom of Guinea.* Translated by Albert van Dantzig and Adam Jones. 1602; New York: British Academy, 1987.

Donnan, Elizabeth, ed. *Documents Illustrative of the History of the Slave Trade to America.* 4 vols. Series no. 409. Washington, D.C.: Carnegie Institute, 1930.

Easterby, James Harold, et al., eds. *Journals of the Commons House of Assembly, 1736–1775.* 21 vols. Columbia: University of South Carolina Press, 1951–1983.

Edgar, Walter, ed. *The Letter book of Robert Pringle.* Columbia: University of South Carolina Press, 1972.

Elliot, William. *Carolina Sports by Land and Water: Including Incidents of Devilfishing. Wild-Cat, Deer, and Bear Hunting Etc.* 1859; Columbia, S.C.: Derby and Jackson, 1994.

Feduccia, Alan, ed. *Catesby's Birds of Colonial America.* Chapel Hill: University of North Carolina Press, 1985.

Grimke, John Fauchereaud, ed. *The Public Laws of South Carolina from Its First Establishment as British Province Down to the Year 1790.* Philadelphia: Aitken and Son, 1790.

Holman, James. *Travels in Madeira, Sierra Leone, Teneriffe, St. Jago, Cape Coast, Fenando Po, Princes Island Etc. Etc.* London: George Routledge, Leicester Square, 1840.

Hudson, Charles, ed. *The Juan Pardo Expeditions: Spanish Explorers and the Indians of the Carolinas and Tennesssee.* Washington, D.C.: Smithsonian Institution Press, 1990.

Hulton, Paul, ed. *The Work of Jacques le Moyne, a Huguenot Artist in France, Florida, and England.* London: British Museum Publications, 1977.

———. *America 1585: The Complete Drawings of John White.* Chapel Hill: University of North Carolina Press, 1984.

Hutchinson, Thomas J. *Ten Years of Wanderings Amongst the Ethiopians: With Sketches of the Manners, Customs, of Civilized and Uncivilized Tribes from Senegal to Gaboon.* London: Hurst and Blacket, 1861.

Johnson, Elmer D., and Kathleen Lewis Sloan, eds. *South Carolina: A Documentary Profile of the Palmetto State.* Columbia: University of South Carolina Press, 1971.

Langley, Clara, ed. *South Carolina Deed Abstracts 1719–1772.* 4 vols. Easely, S.C.: Southern Historical Press, 1983.

Lawson, John, ed. *A New Voyage to South Carolina.* Chapel Hill: University of North Carolina Press, 1967.

Labaree, Leonard Woods, ed. *Royal Instructions to British Governors 1670–1776.* 2 vols. New York: Octagon Books, 1967.

Lewis, Theodore H., ed. *Spanish Explorers of the United States: Original Narratives of Early American History.* New York: Barnes and Noble, 1907.

Mallard, R. Q. *Plantation Life before Emancipation.* Richmond, Va.: Negro History Press, 1892.

McDowell, William L. ed. *Journals of the Commissioners of Indian Trade, 1710–1718.* Columbia: South Carolina Archives Department, 1955.

Moore, Caroline T., and Agatha Simmons, eds. *Abstracts of the Wills of South Carolina, 1670–1740.* Columbia, S.C.: R. L. Bryan Company, 1961.

Radin, Paul, ed. *African Folk Tales and Sculpture.* New York: Bollingen Foundation, 1964.

Rivers, William M., ed. *Historical Sketches of South Carolina.* Charleston, S.C.: McCarter and Company, 1856.

Rogers, George C. Junior, et al., eds. *The Papers of Henry Laurens Papers.* 16 vols. Columbia: University of South Carolina Press, 1972–2001.

Salley, Alexander S. *Journal of the Grand Council of South Carolina.* Columbia: Historical Commission of South Carolina, 1907.

———. *Journal of the Commons House of Assembly.* 21 vols. Columbia: Historical Commission of South Carolina, 1907–1946.

———. *Journals of the Commissioners of the Navy of South Carolina, October 9, 1769–March 1–16, 1779.* Columbia, S.C.: The State Company, 1912.

———. *The Origins of Carolina.* Columbia, S.C.: The State Company, 1926.

———. *Records in British Public Office Relating to South Carolina.* 5 vols. and 31 reels of microfilm. Columbia: Historical Commission of South Carolina, 1928–1946.

———. *Narratives of Early Carolina:1650–1708.* New York: Barnes and Noble, 1967.

———. *Warrants for Land in South Carolina, 1617–1711.* Columbia: University of South Carolina Press, 1973.

Shaw, Janet. *Journal of a Lady of Quality: Being the Narrative of a Journey from Scotland to the West Indies, North Carolina and Portugal, in the years 1774–1776,* edited by Evangeline Walker Andrews. New Haven: University of Nebraska Press, 1921.

Taurinius, Zacharias. *Travels through the interior of Africa, from the Cape of Good Hope to Morocco; in Caffraria, the Kingdoms of Mataman, Angola, Massi, Monoemugi, Muschako, Bahahara, Wangara, Haoussa, &c., &c. and thence through the desert of Sahara and the north of Barbary to Morocco. Between the years 1781 and 1797.* London: R. Philips, 1801.

U.S. Bureau of the Census. *Historical Statistics of the United States Colonial Times to 1957.* Series Z. Washington, D.C.: U.S. Bureau of the Census, 1960.

Van der Broeck, Pieter. *Journal of Voyages to Cape Verde, Guinea, and Angola, 1605–1612.* Translated by J. D. La Fleur. 1634; London: No. 5. Hakluyt Society, 2000.

Web, Edmund James, ed. *Africa as Seen by the Explorers.* London: E. Arnold, 1899.

Secondary Sources

Books, Articles, and Published Reports

Albion, Robert Greenhalgh. *Forests and Seapower: The Timber Problem of the Royal Navy 1652–1862.* Cambridge, Mass.: Harvard University Press, 1926.

Alford, Michael. "Origins of the Carolina Split Dugout Canoes." *International Journal of Nautical Archaeology* 21:3 (1992): 191–203.

———. "The Tool Bag: Periauger, Pettiagua, Petty Puzzler: Kunner, Cooner, Colloquial Conundrum." *Tributaries* (October 2, 1992): 33–34.

Andrews, Charles M. *The Colonial Period of American History: England's Commercial and Colonial Policy.* New Haven: Yale University Press, 1938.

Ascher, Robert, and Charles Fairbanks. "Excavation of a Slave Cabin, Georgia." *Historical Archaeology* 18 (1990): 1–14.

Bailey, Edgar, and Louise, eds. *Biographical Directory of the South Carolina House of Representatives: The Commons House of Assembly, 1692–1775.* Columbia: University of South Carolina Press, 1977.

Bailyn, Bernard. *Voyagers to the West: A Passage in the Peopling of America on the Eve of the Revolution.* New York: Random House, 1986.

Bailyn, Bernard, and Philip Morgan. *Strangers within the Realm: Cultural Margins of the First British Empire.* Chapel Hill: University of North Carolina Press, 1991.

Baker, William A. *Colonial Vessels: Some Seventeenth Century Designs.* Barre, Mass.: Barre Publishing Company, 1962.

———. *Sloops and Shallops.* Columbia: University of South Carolina Press, 1966.

———. "Adventure: A Seventeenth Century Ketch." *American Neptune* 30:2 (April 1970): 81–85.

Baldwin, Agnes. *First Settlers of South Carolina.* Columbia: University of South Carolina Press, 1969.

Barbour, Violet. "Privateers and Pirates of the West Indies." *American Historical Review* 16 (1911): 82–86

Barnwell, Joseph, ed. "Fort King George: Journal of Captain John Barnwell." *South Carolina Historical Magazine* 27 (1926): 189–203.

Barr, William. "Childesbury and Ashley Ferry Town: Elements of Control in the Economic Landscape of Colonial South Carolina." *Underwater Archaeology Proceedings from the Society for Historical Archaeology Conference* (1995): 88–93.

Beard, David. "Causeways and Landings: An Archaeological Study of Riverine Adaptation in South Carolina Lowcountry." In *Historic Landscapes in South Carolina: Historical Archaeological Perspectives of the Land and its People,* edited by Linda F. Stine, Lesley M. Druker, Martha Zeerdan, and Christopher Judge. Charleston: Council of South Carolina Professional Archaeologists, 1993.

Birmingham, David. *Trade and Conflict in Angola: The Mbundu and Their Neighbours under the Influence of the Portuguese, 1483–1790.* Oxford: Clarendon Press, 1966.

Bolster, Jeffrey. *Black Jacks: African American Men in the Age of Sail.* Cambridge, Mass.: Harvard University Press, 1998.

Boxer, Charles. *The Golden Age of Brazil.* Berkeley: University of California Press, 1962.

———. *Four Centuries of Portuguese Expansion.* Berkeley: University of California Press, 1963.

———. *Race Relations in the Portuguese Colonial Empire.* Berkeley: University of California Press, 1963.

Braithwaite, Edward Kamua. *The Development of Creole Society in Jamaica, 1770–1820.* Oxford: Clarendon Press, 1971.

Breunig, Peter. "The 8,000-Year-Old Dugout Canoe from Dufuna (NE Nigeria)." In *Aspects of African Archaeology,* edited by G. Pwiti and R. Soper, 261–468. Papers from the Tenth Congress of the Pan-African Association for Prehistory and Related Studies. Harare: University of Zimbabwe Publications, 1996.

Bridenbaugh, Carl. *Colonial Craftsman.* New York: New York University Press, 1950.

Brown, Daniel, Kathryn Cooper, and Lynn Harris. "The Plantation Boat *Accommodation:* The Historical and Archaeological Investigation of the Maritime Icon of the South, Part 1." *Nautical Research Journal* 56:2 (Summer 2011): 93–114.

Brown, Philip M. "Early Indian Trade in the Development of South Carolina Politics, Economics, and Social Mobility during the Proprietary Period." *South Carolina Historical Magazine* 76 (1975): 118–28.

Burrage, Henry S., ed. *Early English and French Voyages 1534–1608: Original Narratives of Early American History,* vol. 5. New York: C. Scribner, 1906.

Bushman, Richard. *The Refinement of America: Persons, Houses, and Cities.* New York: Knopf, 1992.

Calhoun, Jeanne A., Martha Zierden, and Elizabeth Paysinger. "The Geographic Spread of Charleston's Mercantile Community, 1732–1737." *South Carolina Historical Magazine* 86 (July 1985): 182–220.

Cecelski, David. *The Waterman's Song: Slavery and Freedom in Maritime North Carolina.* Chapel Hill: University of North Carolina Press, 2001.

Chapelle, Howard. *The History of American Sailing Ships.* New York: Bonanza Books, 1935.

Clark, Victor S. *History of the Manufactures in the United States: 1607–1928.* 3 vols. New York: 1948.

Clowse, Converse. *Economic Beginnings in Colonial South Carolina, 1670–1730.* Columbia: University of South Carolina Press, 1971.

———. "Shipowning and Shipbuilding in Colonial South Carolina." *American Neptune* 44:4 (Fall 1984): 221–24.

Coclanis, Peter. "Rice Prices in the 1720s and the Evolution of the South Carolina Economy." *Journal of Southern History* 48 (1982): 531–44.

———. *Shadow of a Dream: Economic Life and Death in the South Carolina Lowcountry, 1670–1920.* New York: Oxford University Press, 1989.

Coker, Priestly C. *Charleston's Maritime Heritage, 1670–1865.* Charleston, S.C.: Coker Craft Press, 1987.

Crane, Verner. *Southern Frontier, 1670–1732.* New York: W. W. Norton, 1981.

Cummins, John. *The Voyage of Christopher Columbus.* New York: St. Martin's Press, 1992.

Curtin, Philip. *The Atlantic Slave Trade: A Census.* Madison: University of Wisconsin, 1969.

Curtin, Philip D., and Jan Vansina. "Sources of the Nineteenth Century Slave Trade." *Journal of African History* 2 (1964): 185–208.

Dawson, Kevin. "Enslaved Swimmers and Divers in the Atlantic World." *Journal of American History* 92:4 (March 2006): 1327–55.

Deas, Anne Simons. *Recollections of the Ball Family of South Carolina (1909) and the Comingtee Plantation.* Spartenburg, S.C.: The Reprint Company, 1978.

Dobson, David. *Directory of Scots in the Carolinas, 1680–1830.* Baltimore: Genealogical Publishing Company, 1986.

Donnan, Elizabeth. "The Slave Trade into South Carolina before the American Revolution." *American Historical Review* 33 (July 1928): 804–28.

Dunn, Richard S. *Sugar and Slaves: The Rise of the Planter Class in the English West Indies, 1624–1713.* Chapel Hill: University of North Carolina Press, 1972.

Edgar, Walter. "Robert Pringle's World." *South Carolina Historical Magazine* 76 (1975): 8–9.

———. *South Carolina: A History.* Columbia: University of South Carolina Press, 1998.

Fairbanks, Charles H. "The Plantation Archaeology of the Southeastern Coast." *Historical Archaeology* 5 (1995): 3–17.

Farr, James Barker. *Black Odyssey: The Seafaring Traditions of African Americans.* New York: Peter Lang, 1991.

Ferguson, Leland. "Slave Settlement and Community Patterns along the East Branch of the Cooper River: Plans for Research." *South Carolina Antiquities* 18:12 (1986): 25–32.

———. *Uncommon Ground: Archaeology and Early African American*. Washington, D.C.: Smithsonian Institution Press, 1992.

Fleetwood, William C. *Tidecraft: The Boats of South Carolina, Georgia and Northeastern Florida, 1550–1950*. Tybee Island, Georgia: W.B.G. Marine Press, 1995.

Ford, Ben. "Down by the Water's Edge: Modelling Shipyard Locations in Maryland, USA." *International Journal of Nautical Archaeology* 36:1 (2007): 125–37.

Frey, Sylvia R. *Water from the Rock: Black Resistance in a Revolutionary Age*. Princeton: Princetown University Press, 1991.

Geggus, David. "Sex Ratio and Ethnicity: A Reply to Paul Lovejoy." *Journal of African History* 30 (1989): 397–99.

Genovese, Eugene. *The World the Slaveholders Made: Two Essays in Interpretation*. New York: Pantheon, 1969.

———. *Roll Jordan Roll: The World the Slaves Made*. Vol. 652. New York: Random House Digital, 1976.

Gilliland, Marion Spjut. *The Material Culture of Key Marco*. Gainesville: University of Florida Press, 1975.

Greene, Jack P. "Colonial South Carolina and the Caribbean Connection." *South Carolina Historical Magazine* 88 (1987): 192–210.

Greene, Jack, and Jack R. Pole, eds. *Colonial British America: Essays in the New History of the Modern Era*. Baltimore: Johns Hopkins University Press, 1984.

Gwynn, Aubrey. "Cromwell's Policy of Transportation." *Irish Quarterly Review* 19 (December 1930): 86–95.

Harper, Lawrence. *The English Navigation Laws*. New York: Columbia University Press, 1939.

Harris, Lynn. "Sea and Swamp Craft: The Utility of Canoe and Canoe Built Vessels in the Lowcountry." *Legacy: The Newsletter of the South Carolina Institute of Archaeology and Anthropology* 2:3 (December 1997): 20–22.

———. "Public Education and Submerged Smallcraft Documentation in South Carolina." *Museum Smallcraft Association Transactions* 3 (1997): 46–53.

———. "Flowing Timelines: Maritime Heritage Trails in South Carolina." *Sandlapper Magazine* (Summer 1999): 812.

Hatley, Thomas. *Dividing Paths: Cherokees and South Carolinians through the Era of the Revolution*. London: Oxford University Press, 1993.

Heyward, Lida, and John Thornton. "African Fiscal Systems as Sources for Demographic History: The Case of Central Angola." *Journal of African History* 29 (1988): 213–28.

Hocker, Frederick M. "The Clydesdale Plantation Project Report: 1992 Field Report." *Institute for Nautical Archaeology Quarterly* 19:4 (1992): 12–16.

———. "The Brown's Ferry Vessel: An Interim Hull Report." *Underwater Archaeology Proceedings from the Society for Historical Archaeology Conference* (1992): 20–25.

Hornell, James. "The Kru Canoes of Sierra Leone." *Mariners Mirror* 15:3 (July 1929): 232–37.

———."African Bark Canoes." *Man* (December 1935): 198, Plate M.

Houmes, Terry, and Gary Houmes. *Bubbling Spring. The Edward Kriegsmann Pritchard Family History: A Direct Line Study*. Charleston, S.C.: Professional Research Publishing Company, 1986.

Hutchins, John B. G. *History and Development of the Shipbuilding Industry.* Cambridge, Mass.: Harvard University Press, 1941.

Ivers, Larry. "Scouting the Inland Passage, 1685–1737." *South Carolina Historical Magazine* 73:3 (July 1972): 117–29.

Jarvis, Michael J. "Maritime Masters and Seafaring Slaves in Bermuda, 1680–1783." *William and Mary Quarterly* 59 (July 2002): 585–682.

Joyner, Charles. *Down by the Riverside: A South Carolina Slave Community.* Urbana: University of Illinois Press, 1984.

———. *Shared Traditions: Southern History and Folk Culture.* Urbana: University of Illinois Press, 1999.

Klein, Herbert S. *The Middle Passage: Comparative Studies in the Atlantic Slave Trade.* Princeton: Princeton University Press, 1978.

Knappert, Jan. *Namibia, Land and Peoples, Myths and Fables.* Leiden, Netherlands: E. J. Brill, 1981.

Law, Robin. "Trade and Politics behind the Slave Coast: The Lagoon Traffic and the Rise of Lagos, 1500–1800." *Journal of African History* 24 (1983): 321–48.

Lawrence, Levine. *Black Culture and Consciousness: Afro American Folk Thought from Slavery to Freedom.* New York: Oxford University Press, 1977.

Lemisch, Jesse. "Jack Tar in the Streets: Merchant Seamen in the Politics of Revolutionary America." *William and Mary Quarterly* 3:25 (1968): 371–407.

Leshikar, Margaret. "Construction of a Dugout Canoe in the Parish of St. Anne, Jamaica." *Proceedings of the Sixteenth Conference on Underwater Archaeology.* Special Publication, Series 4 (1995): 48–51.

Linebaugh, Peter, and Marcus Rediker. *The Many-Headed Hydra: Sailors, Slaves, and Commoners, and the Hidden History of the Revolutionary Atlantic.* Boston: Beacon Press, 2000.

Littlefield, Daniel. *Rice and Slaves: Ethnicity and the Slave Trade in Colonial Carolina.* Baton Rouge: Louisiana State University, 1981.

Long, Edward. *The History of Jamaica.* 3 vols. London: T. Lowdnes, 1974.

MacDonald, George F., and Barbara A. Purdy. "Florida's Wet Sites: Where the Fragile Past Survives." *Early Man* 4 (1982): 6–14.

Mandell, Richard. *Sport: A Cultural History.* New York: iUniverse, 1999.

Mathews, Maurice. "A Contemporary View of South Carolina." *South Carolina Historical Magazine* 55 vol. 3 (1954): 153–59.

McCarthy, Angela, ed. *A Global Clan: Scottish Migrant Networks and Identities since the Eighteenth Century.* London: Tauris Academic Studies, 2006.

McCrady, Edward. *The History of South Carolina under the Royal Government, 1719–1776.* New York: The Macmillan Company, 1899.

McCusker, John, and Russel Menard, eds. *The Economy of British America, 1607–1709.* Chapel Hill: University of North Carolina Press, 1986.

McIver, Petrona. "Early Taverns of the Georgetown Road." *Names in South Carolina* 14 (Winter 1972): 33–34.

Merrens, Roy, ed. *The Colonial South Carolina Scene.* Columbia: University of South Carolina Press, 1977.

Milling, Chapman. *Colonial South Carolina.* Columbia: University of South Carolina Press, 1951.

Minchinton, Walter. "Richard Champion, Nicholas Pocock, and the Carolina Trade." *South Carolina Historical Magazine* 65 (April 1964): 87–97.

Moffatt, Lucius G., and Joseph M. Carriere, eds. "A Frenchman Visits Charleston, 1817." *South Carolina Historical and Genealogical Magazine* 49 (1948): 136–54.

Moore, Warner O. "The Largest Exporters of Deerskins from Charleston, 1735–1775." *South Carolina Historical Magazine* 76 (1975): 144–45.

Morgan, Philip. *Slave Counterpoint: Black Culture in the Eighteenth Century Chesapeake and Lowcountry.* Chapel Hill: University of North Carolina Press, 1998.

Mullin, Michael. *Africa in America: Slave Acculturation and Resistance in the American South.* Urbana: University of Illinois Press, 1992.

Naylor, Carleton. *The Day the Johnboat Went up the Mountain: Stories from My Twenty Years in Maritime Archaeology.* Columbia: University of South Carolina Press, 2010.Neill, Wilfred T. "Dugouts of the Mikasuki Seminole." *Florida Anthropologist* 6:3 (1953): 77–84.

———. "Coracles or Skinboats of the Southeastern Indians." *Florida Anthropologist* 7:4 (1954): 119–26.

Newsome, Lee and Barbara A. Purdy, "Florida Canoes: A Maritime Heritage from the Past." *The Florida Anthropologist* 43:3 (September 1990): 164–80.

Nichols, Patricia Causey. *Voices of Our Ancestors: Language Contact in Early South Carolina.* Columbia: University of South Carolina Press, 2009.

Olsberg, Nicholas. "Ship Registers in the South Carolina Archives, 1734–1780." *South Carolina and Historical and Genealogical Magazine* 74 (October 1973): 189–299.

Olwell, Robert. *Masters, Slaves, and Subjects: The Culture of Power in the South Carolina Lowcountry, 1740–1790.* Ithaca, N.Y.: Cornell University Press, 1998.

Orvin, Maxwell Clayton *Historic Berkeley County, 1671–1900.* Charleston, S.C.: Comprint, 1973.

Pease, William H., and Jane H. Pease. *The Web of Progress: Private Values and Public Styles in Boston and Charleston, 1828–1843.* New York: Oxford University Press, 1985.

Philips, Ulrich B. "The Slave Labor Problem in the Charleston District." *Political Science Quarterly* 22:3 (September 1907): 416–39.

Philips, Ulrich B., ed. *Documentary History of American Industrial Society.* Cleveland: Arthur H. Clark Company, 1910.

Powers, Bernard E. *Black Charlestonians: A Social History,* 1822–1885. Fayetteville: University of Arkansas Press, 1994.

Price, Richard. "Caribbean Fishing and Fishermen: A Historical Sketch." *American Anthropologist* 78 (1968): 1363–83.

Quigley, Carroll. "Aboriginal Fish Poisons and the Diffusion Problem." *American Anthropologist* 58 (1956): 508–25.

Richardson, David. "Slave Exports from West and West Central Africa from 1700–1810." *Journal of African History* 30 (1989): 1–2.

Rediker, Marcus. *Between the Devil and the Deep Blue Sea: Merchant Seamen, Pirates, and the Anglo- American World, 1700–1750.* Cambridge: Cambridge University Press, 1987.

Salas, Antonio, Ángel Carracedo, Martin Richards, and Vincent Macaulay. "Charting the Ancestry of African Americans." *American Journal of Human Genetics* 77:4 (October 2005): 676–80.

Salas, Antonio, Martin Richards, María-Victoria Lareu, Rosaria Scozzari, Alfredo Coppa, Antonio Torroni, Vincent Macaulay, and Ángel Carracedo. "The African Diaspora: Mitochondrial DNA and the Atlantic Slave Trade."*American Journal of Human Genetics* 74:3 (March 2004): 454–65.

Sellars, Leila. *Charleston Business on the Eve of the Revolution.* Chapel Hill: University of North Carolina Press, 1934.

Sheppard, Jill. *The Redlegs of Barbadoes.* Millwood, N.Y.: KTO Press, 1977.

Sheridan, Richard. *Sugar and Slavery: An Economic History of the British West Indies.* Baltimore: Johns Hopkins University Press, 1973.

Smelser, Marshall, and William I. Davisson. "The Longevity of Colonial Ships." *American Neptune* 33:1 (January 1973): 17–19.

Smith, David. "Dependent Urbanization in Colonial America: The Case of Charleston, South Carolina." *Social Forces* 66:1 (September 1987): 1–28.

Smith, Henry A. M. "Childesbury." *South Carolina Historical and Genealogical Magazine* 15 (1914): 107–12.

———. "The Orange Quarter and the First French Settlers in South Carolina." *South Carolina Historical and Genealogical Magazine* 18 (1917): 101–23.

———. "French Town." *South Carolina Historical and Genealogical Magazine* 72 (1971): 220–27.

Smith, Roger. "The Canoe in West African History." *Journal of African History* 4 (1970): 515–33.

Sommerville, Keith. *Angola: Politics, Economics and Society.* Boulder, Colo.: Lynne Reiner, 1986.

Speake, Jennifer. *Literature of Travel and Exploration.* 3 vols. New York: Taylor and Francis, 2003.

Starbuck, Alexander. *History of the American Whale Fishery from Its Earliest Inception to the Year 1876*, Castle, New York, 1989.

Steele, Ian. *The English Atlantic, 1675–1746.* New York: Oxford University Press, 1986.

Steffy, Richard J. "Hull Construction Features of the Brown's Ferry Vessel." (South Carolina Institute of Archaeology and Anthropology) *Notebook* 10 (1978), 1–29.

———. *Wooden Ship Building and the Interpretation of Shipwrecks.* College Station: Texas A&M University Press, 1994.

———."The Thirteen Colonies: English Settlers and Seafarers." In *Ships and Shipwrecks of the Americas,* edited by G. F. Bass. New York: Thames and Hudson, 1988.

Stephenson, Robert, ed. "A Dugout Canoe from Sumter County." (South Carolina Institute of Archaeology and Anthropology) *Notebook* 12 (December 1980): 23–26.

Stoller, Lincoln. "The Indian's Apprentice." *Wooden Boat* 74 (January–February 1987): 27–33.

Stoney, Samuel Gaillard and William John Grayson, "The Autobiography of William John Grayson," *South Carolina Historical and Genealogical Magazine* 49 (January 1948): 25.

Stumpf, Stuart O. "Implications of King George's War for the Charleston Mercantile Community." *South Carolina Historical Magazine* 77 (July 1976): 161–88.

Swanton, John. "Indians of the South Eastern United States." *Bureau of American Ethnology Bulletin* 27 (1946): 263–338.

Terry, George D. *Champaign Country: A Social History of an Eighteenth Century Lowcountry Parish in South Carolina, St. Johns, Berkeley County*. Columbia: University of South Carolina Press, 1981.

Thomas, John P. "The Barbadians in Early South Carolina." *South Carolina Historical and Genealogical Magazine* 31 (April 1930): 75–92.

Thornton, John. "Demography and History in the Kingdom of Kongo, 1550–1750." *Journal of African History* 18 (1977): 507–31.

Tower, W. S. *A History of the American Whale Fishers*. Philadelphia: University of Pennsylvania Press, 1907.

Turner, Grace. "Bahamian Ship Grafitti." *International Journal of Nautical Archaeology* 35:2 (2006): 253–73.

Uya, Okan Eder. *From Slavery to Public Service: Robert Smalls, 1839–1915*. New York: Oxford University Press, 1971.

Verrips, Jojada. "Ghaniain Canoe Decorations." *Maritime Studies* 1:1 (2002): 43–66.

Waddell, Gene. *Indians of the South Carolina Lowcountry, 1562–1751*. Spartenburg, S.C.: The Reprint Company, 1974.

———. "Ignorance and Deceit in Renaming Charleston's Rivers, Some Observations about the Reliability of Historical Sources." *South Carolina Historical Magazine* 89 (January 1988): 40–50.

Walsh, Richard. *Charleston's Sons of Liberty*. Columbia: University of South Carolina Press, 1961.

Ward, Albert, ed. *Forgotten Places and Things: Archaeological Perspectives on American History*. Columbia: University of South Carolina Press, 1983.

Waterhouse, Richard. *A New World Gentry: The Making of the Merchant and Planter Class in South Carolina, 1670–1770*. New York: Garland Press, 1989.

Wax, Donald. "Preferences for Slaves in Colonial America." *Journal of Negro History* 57 (March 1978): 371–401.

Weber, Mabel. "The Bond Family of Hobcaw Plantation, Christchurch Parish." *South Carolina Historical and Genealogical Magazine* 25 (January 1925): 10–11.

———. "Josiah Smith's Diary, 1780–1781." *South Carolina Historical and Genealogical Magazine* 34 (October 1933): 194–210.

Weir, Robert M. *Colonial South Carolina*. Millwood, N.Y.: KTO Press, 1983.

Wiggins, David. "Leisure Time on Southern Plantations: The Slaves' Respite from Constant Toil, 1810–1860." In *Sport in America: New Historical Perspectives*, edited by Donald Spivey. Westport, Conn.: Greenwood Press, 1985.

Wilbanks, Ralph. "A Progress Report on Small Watercraft-based Research Projects in South Carolina." (South Carolina Institute of Archaeology and Anthropology) *Notebook* 12:3–4 (July–December 1980): 17–27.

Wilkie, Laurie. "Glass-Knapping at a Louisiana Plantation: African American Too." *Journal of the Society of Historical Archaeology* 30:4 (1996): 37–49.

Williams, J. *Whence the Black Irish of Jamaica*. New York: Dial Press, 1932.

Windley, Lathan, ed. *Runaway Slave Advertisements: A Documentary History from the 1730s to 1790s*. 4 vols. Westport, Conn.: Greenwood Press 1983.Wood, Peter. *Black Majority:*

Negroes in Colonial South Carolina from 1670 through the Stono Rebellion. New York: W.W. Norton, 1974.

Wood, Virginia Steele. *Live Oaking: Southern Timber for Tall Ships.* Boston: Northeastern University Press, 1981.

Zierden, Martha, Leslie Drucker, and Jeanne Calhoun. *Home Upriver: Rural Life on Daniel's Island, Berkley County, SC,* vol. 1. Carolina Archaeological Services, South Carolina Department of Highways and Public Transportation, 1996.

Unpublished Secondary Materials

Albright, Alan. "Electronic Survey of Archaeological Sites in Certain Rivers in South Carolina." South Carolina Institute of Archaeology and Anthropology, University of South Carolina, Columbia, no date.

Amer, Christopher, and Bruce Thompson. "The Little Landing Survey, Cooper River, South Carolina." South Carolina Institute of Archaeology and Anthropology, University of South Carolina, Columbia, 1989.

Amer, Christopher, et al. "The Malcolm Boat (38BK803): Discovery Stabilization, and Preservation of a Historic Seagoing Smallcraft in the Ashley River." Research Manuscript, no. 217. South Carolina Institute of Archaeology and Anthropology, University of South Carolina, Columbia, 1997.

Barr, William. "Strawberry Ferry and Childesbury Towne: A Socio-Economic Enterprise on the West Branch of the Cooper River, Berkeley County, St. Johns Parish, South Carolina." Master's thesis, University of South Carolina, 1995.

Beta Analytic. "Report of Radio Carbon Dating Analysis." Letter dated May 1999. On file at Charleston Field Office, South Carolina Institute of Archaeology and Anthropology.

Eliades, David K. "The Indian Policy of Colonial South Carolina, 1670–1763." Ph.D. dissertation, University of South Carolina, 1981.

Errante, James. "Waterscape Archaeology: A Survey for 18th-Century Boat Landings at Middleburg Plantation, Berkeley County, South Carolina." Master's thesis, University of South Carolina, 1993.

Friedlander, Amy E. "Carolina Huguenots: A Study in Colonial Pluralism." Ph.D. dissertation, Emory University, 1979.

Gray, Allison Winnifred. "Canoe Decoration and Meaning amongst the Fante of the Cape Coast." *African Diaspora Collection,* School for International Training (SIT), Graduate Institute/SIT Study Abroad, 1996.

Harris, Lynn. "The Waccamaw-Richmond Hill Waterfront Project 1991: Laurel Hill Barge No. 2." Research Manuscript no. 214, Stephenson Award Series. South Carolina Institute of Archaeology and Anthropology, University of South Carolina, Columbia, 1992.

———. "The Ashley River Survey." South Carolina Institute of Archaeology and Anthropology, University of South Carolina, Columbia, 1996.

Harris, Lynn, Jimmy Moss, and Carl Naylor. "The Cooper River Survey: An Underwater Reconnaissance of the West Branch." Research Manuscript no. 218. South Carolina Institute of Archaeology and Anthropology, University of South Carolina, Columbia, 1993.

Harris, Lynn, and Tina Rust. "Archaeological Investigations at the Hobcaw Shipyard Site, South Eastern Archaeology and History." Technical Report submitted to South Carolina State Historic Preservation Office, Charleston, 2004.

Harris, Lynn, Tina Rust, and Monica Beck. "Archaeological Excavations at the Hobcaw Shipyard Site, South Eastern Archaeology and History." Technical Report submitted to South Carolina State Historic Preservation Office, Charleston, 2005.

Hicks, Theresa. "Wharves: The Keystone of Plantation Wealth? Case Studies." Master's thesis, East Carolina University, 2012.

Hocker, Frederick M. "The Place of the Brown's Ferry Vessel in the Evolution of the Flat Bottomed Boat." Texas A&M University, College Station, 1985.

Lesnick, Edward Charles. "A Quantitive Analysis of the Supply and Demand for Ships: A Case Study of Colonial New York and Carolina." Ph.D. dissertation, University of Notre Dame, 1973.

Linder, Suzanne. "River in Time: A Cultural Study of Yadkin Pee Dee System to 1825." Ph.D. dissertation, University of South Carolina, 1993.

Manning, Kathy. "Water Travel of the Southeastern Indians." Paper presented at the Thirty-sixth Annual Meeting of the Southeastern Archaeological Conference at the University of Georgia. South Carolina Institute of Archaeology and Anthropology files, University of South Carolina, 1979.

Marin, Craig. "Following the Water: The Resistance Activities of Slave Boatmen in South Carolina and Georgia, 1732–1800." Master's thesis, University of Pittsburgh, 1998.

Morby, Sarah. "Pritchard Shipyard: A Landscape Analysis of South Carolina's Largest Colonial and Antebellum Shipyard." Master's thesis, University of South Carolina, 2000.

Newell, Mark. "Historic Working Smallcraft of South Carolina." South Carolina Institute of Archaeology and Anthropology, University of South Carolina, Columbia, 1986.

———. "Historic Working Smallcraft of South Carolina: A Preliminary Typology." South Carolina Institute of Archaeology and Anthropology, University of South Carolina, Columbia, 1991.

———. "Historic Working Smallcraft of South Carolina: Barges, Flats and Ferries." South Carolina Institute of Archaeology and Anthropology, University of South Carolina, Columbia, 1991a.

———. "The Historic Working Craft of South Carolina: A General Typology with a Study of Adaptations of Flatboat Design." Research Manuscript no.7. Georgia Archaeological Institute, Augusta, 1996.

Newell, Mark, and Simmons, Joe. "The Santee Canal Sanctuary. Part 1." South Carolina Institute of Archaeology and Anthropology, University of South Carolina, Columbia, 1989.

Nylund, Rowena. "The Historical Background of the Brown's Ferry Vessel." Master's thesis, University of South Carolina, 1989.

O'Neil, Nicola. "The Coastal Fishing Canoes of Ghana." Master's thesis, Scottish Institute of Maritime Studies, St. Andrews University, 1991.

Pecorelli, Harry III. "Archaeological Investigations of the B&B Plantation Wreck (38BK1762): An Eighteenth-Century Plantation Vessel, Charleston, South Carolina." Master's thesis, East Carolina University, 2003.

Poplin, Eric. "Expedient Technology in European North America; Implications of an Alternate use of Glass by Historic Period Populations." Ph.D. dissertation, University of Calgary, 1986.

Smith, Shelley E. "The Plantations of Colonial South Carolina: Transmission and Transformation in Provincial Culture." Ph.D. dissertation, Columbia University, 1999.

Snell, William R. "Indian Slavery in Colonial South Carolina, 1671–1795." Ph.D. dissertation, University of Alabama, 1972.

Stavisky, Leonard Price. "The Negro Artisan in the South Atlantic States, 1800–1860: A Study of Status and Economic Opportunity with Special Reference to Charleston." Ph.D. dissertation, Columbia University, 1958.

Vezeau, Susan Lynn. "The Mepkin Abbey Shipwreck: Diving into South Carolina's Plantation Past." Master's thesis, Texas A&M University, 2004.

Wilbanks, Ralph. "The Roots Site: A Post-Contact Canoe." South Carolina Institute of Archaeology and Anthropology, University of South Carolina, Columbia.

Index